HUMAN CHOICE IN INTERNATIONAL LAW

Human Choice in International Law is an exploration of human choice in international legal and political decision making. This book investigates the neurobiology of how people choose and the history of how personal choice has affected decisions about international peace and security. It charts important decision moments in international law about genocide, intervention into armed conflict and nuclear weapons at the central institutions of the international legal order. Professor Spain Bradley analyzes the role that particular individuals, serving as international judges or Security Council representatives, play in shaping decision outcomes and then applies insights from neuroscience to assert the importance of analyzing how cognitive processes such as empathy, emotion and bias can influence such decision makers. Drawing upon historical accounts and personal interviews, this book reveals the beauty and struggle of human influences that shape the creation and practice of international law.

Anna Spain Bradley is Vice Chancellor of Equity, Diversity and Inclusion and Professor of Law at University of California, Los Angeles. She is an award-winning international law scholar, educator and expert specializing in international dispute resolution, international human rights and combating global racism. A Vice President of the American Society of International Law, she received the Society's Francis Lieber Prize for excellence in scholarship and is the recipient of the OZY Educator Award. A graduate of Harvard Law School, Spain Bradley has previously served as an Attorney-Adviser at the US Department of State, a US delegate and a Legal Expert to the United Nations, and counsel for state parties before the Permanent Court of Arbitration. She is a member of the Council on Foreign Relations and is a founding member of Mediators Beyond Borders International.

Human Choice in International Law

ANNA SPAIN BRADLEY

University of California, Los Angeles

CAMBRIDGE
UNIVERSITY PRESS

University Printing House, Cambridge CB2 8BS, United Kingdom

One Liberty Plaza, 20th Floor, New York, NY 10006, USA

477 Williamstown Road, Port Melbourne, VIC 3207, Australia

314–321, 3rd Floor, Plot 3, Splendor Forum, Jasola District Centre, New Delhi – 110025, India

103 Penang Road, #05–06/07, Visioncrest Commercial, Singapore 238467

Cambridge University Press is part of the University of Cambridge.

It furthers the University's mission by disseminating knowledge in the pursuit of education, learning, and research at the highest international levels of excellence.

www.cambridge.org
Information on this title: www.cambridge.org/9781108422567
DOI: 10.1017/9781108524957

First published 2021

A catalogue record for this publication is available from the British Library.

Library of Congress Cataloging-in-Publication Data
NAMES: Spain Bradley, Anna, 1978– author.
TITLE: Human choice in international law / Anna Spain Bradley, University of California, Los Angeles.
DESCRIPTION: Cambridge, United Kingdom ; New York, NY : Cambridge University Press, 2021. | Includes index.
IDENTIFIERS: LCCN 2021024609 (print) | LCCN 2021024610 (ebook) | ISBN 9781108422567 (hardback) | ISBN 9781108435550 (paperback) | ISBN 9781108524957 (ebook)
SUBJECTS: LCSH: International law – Decision making.
CLASSIFICATION: LCC KZ1249 .S63 2021 (print) | LCC KZ1249 (ebook) | DDC 341–dc23
LC record available at https://lccn.loc.gov/2021024609
LC ebook record available at https://lccn.loc.gov/2021024610

ISBN 978-1-108-42256-7 Hardback
ISBN 978-1-108-43555-0 Paperback

To my husband, Adam, and my daughters, Ava and Amaya, who remind me of the joys and promise of embracing all that makes us human.

Contents

Figures

Acknowledgments

Writing a book is a labor of love and this book is rooted in my deep love of international law and of humanity. I wish to acknowledge and thank the many people who gave their time and insights to this book in its many forms over the years.

I am indebted to the wisdom and generosity of those individuals who permitted me to interview them for this book, including former and current International Court of Justice judges Professor Georges Abi-Saab, Professor Thomas Buergenthal, Judge Joan Donoghue, and Professor and Judge Bruno Simma as well as renowned international arbitrators Professor Laurence Boisson de Chazournes and Professor Lucy Reed. My deep appreciation to the officials who served at the UN Security Council as well as several other UN experts who shared their experiences, without attribution, with me.

The ideas that became this book were enriched by the generous feedback and insights of many including my international law colleagues Jean d' Aspremont, Tomer Broude, Mary Ellen O'Connell, Harlan Cohen, M.J. Durkee, Susan Franck, Jean Galbraith, Nienke Grossman, Won Kidane, Timothy Meyer, and Catherine Powell; my University of Colorado Law School colleagues Alexia Brunet Marks, Sarah Krakoff, Peter Huang, Pierre Schlag, and University of Colorado neuroscience colleagues Dr. R. McKell Carter and Dr. Sukumar Vijayaraghavan. My ideas for this book blossomed through the insights of participants in attendance at various workshops hosted by the Federal Administrative Law Judges Annual Conference, Geneva Graduate Institute of International and Development Studies, University of Washington Law School, the American Society of International Law, the University of Colorado Law School, and the University of Colorado Institute of Cognitive Science. I am grateful to Grace and Gordon Gamm for the Gamm Justice Award that supported my research.

I would not have written this book, become an international law professor, or become a lawyer without great mentors including three incredible women who changed the course of my career: Carmen Suro-Bredie, Margo Oge, and Avis Robinson. I am grateful for the friendship and encouragement of many others, especially the Reverend Mary Kate Rejouis.

For endless hours assisting with research, citation checks, and good humor, I am endlessly indebted to my former students and research assistants Andrea Savage, Marissa Kardon Weber, and Kehinde O. Winful. Thank you to Jane Thompson and Matt Zafiratos of the University of Colorado Law Library for gracious and exacting research assistance and to Ann Stockho for fine editing.

To all at Cambridge University Press who brought this book to fruition, particularly John Berger, who saw promise in the initial project, and his colleagues Jackie Grant, Catherine Smith, Helen Baxter, and Allan Alphonse, thank you.

Finally, I am forever grateful to my family for support and encouragement that made the impossibility of finishing a book during a global pandemic more possible: my parents, Mary and Bill Spain, my sister and constant cheerleader, Dr. Sarah Spain Shelton, and my most faithful adviser, my husband, Dr. Adam F. Bradley. People make the world go around and you did that for me.

PART I

1

Introduction

A conscientious writer must direct his suggestions to what, after careful examination of political reality, may be considered as being possible tomorrow, although it, perhaps, seems not yet possible today. Otherwise, there would be no hope for progress.

Hans Kelsen[1]

1.1 Child in Gaza. Credit: Abid Katib/Staff/Getty Images

Some years ago, I was invited to a fancy dinner in an elegant city full of international law elites. Gathered at the table were a few current and former judges from international courts, a famous international arbitrator or two, renowned international legal scholars, and the odd family member. The mood was celebratory and the wine flowed. Conversations in French, German, Spanish, and English hung in the air above the long, candlelit table. As a guest of an invited guest, I was not an insider, so I played the part of eager and respectful listener. At least until the end of the evening.

As the dessert cheese arrived, we shuffled seats and I ended up next to the guest of honor, whom I shall call Z. Our polite conversation soon escalated into tense debate. We were discussing the International Court of Justice (ICJ) and its tricky role in interpreting international law within the confines of each case while also upholding fundamental principles of justice. I voiced my disappointment in the ICJ's history of dealing with the crime of genocide.

Things got heated when our conversation turned to the case that the Democratic Republic of the Congo (DRC) brought against Rwanda in 2002. The DRC alleged that Rwanda had committed "massive, serious and flagrant violations of human rights and of international humanitarian law," including genocide along the border between the two nations.[2] If the allegations were true, it meant that Rwanda had become the perpetrator of genocide only a decade or so after people there were its victim. The ICJ decided that it lacked the jurisdiction to hear the case on the merits based on various important but complex legal grounds having to do with Rwanda taking reservations to the Genocide Convention.[3]

Although well-reasoned, the court's decision struck me and many others as a moral abdication. How could the ICJ – the World Court – not have jurisdiction to hear a case alleging the most serious of all international crimes? Z, however, held steadfast that the court had reached the proper decision.

"But it's genocide!" I said, pressing my case. "Didn't that matter? Didn't that upset you?"

Z responded that any emotions that ICJ judges had about the case were inconsequential. The court decided the case in the best way it could based on available law.

"What would you have the court do?" Z asked me in a tone of barely disguised exasperation.

I decided to drop the matter. After all, Z was a sitting judge on the International Court of Justice.

Although I had no way of knowing it then, this book was born that night over dinner. My disagreement with Z stayed with me and I started to question the near-universal assumption that law and emotion must be kept apart. You see, Z believed, as do many judges, arbitrators, diplomats, lawyers, and other elite decision makers in international law, that an individual in such a role can choose to be impartial. That people should – and are able to – set aside any personal convictions, beliefs, feelings, and biases when deciding a case, relying solely on the applicable law and facts before them. I know this because it is what some decision makers have stated or shared.[4] It is also what I, alongside many other students, was taught during the first year of law school. To think like a lawyer means approaching matters with rational thought and a "cool" head.

The origins of this prevailing view, that passions are the enemy of good lawyering and judging, are often attributed to Aristotle.[5] In writing about whether "the best law or the best man should rule"[6] and how a ruler should make decisions, Aristotle claims that "the rule of law is preferable to that of any individual," and "[o]n the same principle, even if it be better for certain individuals to govern, they should be made only guardians and ministers of the law."[7] It was in this context that his now famous words "[t]he law is reason unaffected by desire" appear.[8] This Aristotelian view has prevailed over time and throughout many legal traditions. International law is no exception.

But is this idea, that humans can put aside emotion, empathy, bias, and beliefs when making choices, accurate? More than that, is it even possible? Is there any basis in science for the assumption that we can remain in full control of our thoughts and decisions? Can elite decision makers in international law (and elsewhere) make judgments, assessments, and other choices by rational thinking, divorced from feeling or belief? Moreover, why does this yet unproven idea persist?

My observations in my career and in my life leave me skeptical. Whether as a young assistant at the US Environmental Protection Agency observing a high-level multilateral negotiation, a State Department lawyer turned US delegate at the United Nations in Geneva, or as legal counsel to a state party in international arbitral proceedings at the Permanent Court of Arbitration in The Hague, I have been privy to high-level decision making by international law elites. Factors other than reason were always at play. On the bench or around the negotiating table, people present their professional selves. But then they go home. They live. Their lived experience creates empathy, fear, love, and bias. These factors are ever present, in their brains and within their bodies, when they are making judgments, decisions, assessments, and findings.

My investigations as a scholar support this skepticism. As this book explores, evidence-based insights from neuroscience, cognitive science, and related research reveal that human cognition and human choice are complex endeavors.[9] We cannot simply choose to ignore our emotions or other Aristotelian desires when we engage in cognitive activity that produces a choice.[10] Of course, we can't blame Aristotle. Neuroscience didn't exist back then.[11] But we can use new knowledge to update old ideas and to recognize that human choice is more complex than international law presently takes into account. This is the aim and ambition of this book.

STUDYING HUMAN CHOICE IN INTERNATIONAL LAW

We humans are inherently complex creatures. In the past few decades, research has emerged that reveals just how complex we are. Work in fields such as neuroscience, cognitive studies, psychology, and behavioral economics has led to a fuller understanding of humans, our brains, and our behavior.

Herein, the study of human choice is illuminating how we make the choices we do.[12] We now know that there is no unitary process in our brain for making a choice. Instead, we can invoke different parts of our brain at different times. The cognitive processes we employ to reach a choice may invoke our emotions, experiences, and memories. In other words, choice is much more than the product of thought or judgment. We also know that people tend to make irrational choices in ways that are predictable. Explicit bias and implicit bias are real. Insights like these reveal that human choice is more complex than previously understood. Such new knowledge helps us refine old ideas about who we are and how we decide.

I believe that scientific knowledge about human choice can and should inform the study and practice of international law.[13] Accordingly, this book's central purpose is to introduce the study of human choice to the study and practice of international law. There are existing inquiries into decision making and human behavior in international law that have employed insights from behavioral science, psychology, sociology, mathematics, and computer science.[14] The novelty of this project is that it focuses on understanding human choice through neuroscience, in addition to these aforementioned disciplines.

To do so, the book introduces to international law insights and evidence from neuroscience and cognitive studies about how human beings make choices in the brain. Herein, I first investigate how people make choices, employing neuroscience research that relies on brain-imaging studies and animal studies; research from psychology, which utilizes clinical research with human subjects; behavioral science; and more, which I explain in further detail in Chapter 2.

Next, I aim to bridge knowledge about human choice to understanding how people, serving in elite roles in international legal spaces, create and shape international law through the choices they make. This includes the fifteen people who serve as judges at the ICJ in The Hague, the twelve representatives who sit around the semi-circular table at the UN Security Council in New York City, and powerful political leaders, diplomats, and staff who serve unseen yet important roles in key global organizations. Herein, I engage existing conversations in international law, international relations and decision-making literatures. This includes the examination of decision-making practices of international legal actors in certain contexts such as international courts or the United Nations,[15] explorations of state behavior and international law through a variety of methodologies,[16] and investigations into the very nature of what international law is.[17] This human-choice approach considers how those operating under the imprimatur of international law influence what it is.

Throughout this book, my frame of analysis utilizes scientific insights about human choice and then asks what international law should make of the evidence, not the other way around. International legal scholarship commonly considers how international law affects people. This book frames the conversation around understanding how people affect and shape international law. In aiming to bring the study of human choice and the study of international law together, I acknowledge – indeed, affirm – that there are many areas of relevant inquiry that I do not cover. The study of human choice is vast, as is the study of international law. Space is limited and readers' attention is finite. I ask more questions that I can answer and future scientific breakthroughs will continue to update what is known. These caveats aside, I hope the pages that follow will provide a solid scientific foundation for understanding the rich complexities of human choice and compelling insights into how such complexities shape international law.

FOUNDATIONS, ASSUMPTIONS, AND IMPLICATIONS

Any book about international law should be clear about how it conceives international law. As I define it here, international law is a set of enforceable rules that nations, referred to hereafter as states, have consented to uphold and to be bound to follow.[18] These rules govern relations between states, such as the general prohibition on the use of force, and create rights owed to and obligations owed by states.[19] Historically, states are seen as the central actors in international law.[20]

International law is also more than this. It is a legal system comprised of norms, beliefs, policy, politics, and institutions.[21] International law is the outcome or product of the decision-making processes by which it was made.[22] Here, I extend the view taken by former President of the ICJ, Judge Rosalyn Higgins that, "international law is the entire decision-making process ... made by authorized persons or organs, in appropriate forums, within the framework of certain established practices and norms."[23] International law is all these things: a set of rules, a legal system with norms, and the result of decision-making processes.[24]

International law involves people. In this book, I argue that whatever else international law is, it is also inextricably linked to human choice. To some, this assertion may seem self-evident. Of course, people make law. Legal process theorists have long argued such. Here, I take these instincts and insight further. At every turn, international law involves the choices certain people take, making a human-choice approach to international law valuable. I use the term *choice* to describe the diverse array of brain activity involved in choosing, which includes thought, decision making, judgment, assessment, and more.[25] Choice occurs when a person, serving as a judge, determines the meaning of a general principle to decide if the crime of genocide has occurred. Choice occurs when a diplomat relies on international law, alongside political considerations, when deciding the terms of a trade deal. Choice occurs when heads of state decide to create and enter into a human rights treaty, perhaps influenced by advocates, activists, and public opinion. Even when nations decide, those decisions are made by people acting as agents of the state.

A human-choice approach to understanding international law disrupts commitments to old and outdated understandings. For example, this book asks us once again to question the prevailing view that international law is the product of state behavior. It asks us to reconsider continued reliance on a realist account of international law that often employs rational-choice theory to understand state behavior.[26]

More fundamentally, this project brings the study of international law into better alignment with the study of human behavior. A human-choice analysis of international law reveals why we no longer need to treat international law as if it were superhuman. Instead, we may come to see that legal rules come about because of a caring ambassador or an angry legal advisor or a brilliant but tired lawyer who has kids and only had five hours of sleep last night. We understand that it is not just nations but particular political administrations that are responsible for grave breaches of international law, such as the Bush administration's invasion of Iraq, or Iraq's illegal invasion of Kuwait under Saddam Hussein. Rarely do we speak of these events as being the outcome of choices made by particular people at a particular moment in time. But they are. And we should.

This book's final and most important aim is educational. Centering human choice as an integral part of what international law is places people at the heart of the story. It calls for a cultural shift in how scholars and practitioners understand and take part in the field of international law. By clarifying the scientific realities of human choice, this book hopes to humanize international law and illustrate how law is shaped by the people empowered to make it. By retrieving the human dimension of choice, this book asserts the normality of emotions and beliefs, alongside thought, in the hallowed halls of international legal institutions. These insights ask us to destigmatize all that makes us human.

ORGANIZATION OF THE BOOK

In the chapters that follow, I explain how human choice works, based on scientific evidence and insights, and why such information is relevant to understanding what international law both is and, perhaps more important, can become. The book contains eight chapters, divided among three parts. Part I lays the foundation and framework for the book's central claim that human choice shapes international law.

Chapter 2 presents the book's central thesis – that whatever else international law is, it is also human choice – through a close consideration of the human choices that led to the creation, use, and permissible legality of nuclear weapons. This inside story illustrates that international law and human history have been shaped by choices that a particular person made at a particular moment in time. Human choice has played a significant, yet underexamined, role in shaping international law. The chapter concludes by situating this analysis within relevant theories and frameworks of choice in international law.

Chapter 3 explores the scientific research investigating human choice. It introduces key findings on the ways that thought, empathy, emotion, and bias inform human cognition associated with choice. The chapter offers a neuroscience-driven framework for understanding human choice, while also considering key insights from cognitive studies, psychology, and related fields. It then considers how this evidence-based reality might challenge existing understandings and theories of decision making in international law.

Part II of the book grounds this human-choice approach in three contexts of international legal decision making: the ICJ, or World Court; the UN Security Council; and human rights. Chapter 4 considers how people who serve on the ICJ make their judgments. As the judicial arm of the United Nations, the ICJ is one of the most powerful institutions in the world. Established in 1945, it shapes international law through judicial opinions that decide legal disputes submitted by nations throughout the world. In each case, some dealing with incredibly complex and charged topics concerning genocide or the legality of nuclear weapons, the court's judgment is determined by the choices made by the fifteen women and men who serve on the court. This chapter offers a close examination of decision making at the ICJ at the individual level through a combination of historical analysis and original interviews with current and former ICJ judges. It also considers the *DRC* v. *Rwanda* genocide case and discusses how the court's majority opinion in that case was at odds with the separate opinion. Insights from judges, who discuss candidly how they make legal choices, deepen and contextualize the chapter's analysis and illustrate how judges are subject to the same cognitive limits and possibilities that impact us all.

Chapter 5 examines the human elements of decision making at the UN Security Council. Drawing on interviews with council personnel, it recounts key decision moments including the council's authorization of the use of force in Libya and reveals how decision makers were influenced by their values and beliefs. The chapter then connects such decisions to research on the cognitive aspects of choice in our brains. Analyzing such key council decisions through a cognitive lens better enables us to appreciate how law and norms influence those tasked with making tough decisions about international peace and security.

Chapter 6 analyzes elements of human choice by international legal decision makers in a variety of human-rights contexts. Specifically, I consider how emotion is, perhaps, more accepted in these spaces and examine how emotive dynamics may influence legal choices in human rights. The chapter further explores how to think about fear, shame, and bias alongside compassion and kindness in an area of international law that, by design, exists to uphold the values of dignity, freedom, equality and nondiscrimination.

Part III of the book considers the implications and limitations of a human-choice approach to international law. Chapter 7 argues for a culture shift in international law that better aligns the duties and expectations international law requires with the realities of human choice. I discuss how professional cultures and expectations in international law may ask too much or too little of decision makers by remaining uninformed about human choice. I then consider what embracing human realities such as empathy, emotion, and bias might mean for the culture of international law and consider potential benefits and challenges. The chapter concludes by sketching out new approaches to international legal decision making that could shift the culture of choice in a better direction.

The book concludes in Chapter 8 by considering how we get from the international law we have to the international law we will need in the future. As an instrument for international peace, security, and cooperation, international law has long relied on an international order based on the authority of states. Yet, current and future threats including those arising from climate change, pandemics, cyberwarfare, and terrorism, create challenges that international law is, at present, ill-equipped to meet. These and other future realities call on international law to evolve to be capable of directly engaging the needs and interests of people in addition to states. This chapter takes up these questions in three time periods: international law as it was, international law as it is, and international law as it needs to be. The concluding message is that in order for international law to evolve, those within it need to evolve with it. Understanding human choice dimensions of decision making in international law helps us reimagine the international law we need for our future world.

Human Choice in International Law asks us to rethink what international law is and should be, taking full account of human realities. It initiates an overdue conversation about the tensions between being human, with all its glories and its faults, and being a part of the culture of international law. My hope is that this book will inform, engage, and spark curiosity in those who practice and study international law. Sometimes, in order to understand something more fully or differently, we must take a step back to look at it anew.

International Law as Human Choice

The fate of the world will be such as the world deserves.
Albert Einstein[1]

2.1 Atomic Dome in Hiroshima. Credit: Thomas D. McAvoy/Contributor/Getty Images

"A LONG NOCTURNAL JOURNEY"[2]

On July 8, 1996, the world awoke to a landmark advisory opinion from the International Court of Justice (ICJ): "Nations are not prohibited from using or threatening to use nuclear weapons under international law." Less than two years prior, and after decades of concern about the harm that the existence of nuclear weapons could do to the world, the UN General Assembly had requested that the ICJ provide an advisory opinion on the following question: "Is the threat or use of nuclear weapons in any circumstance permitted under international law?"[3]

The answer they received was unsatisfactory. Media headlined the news as "International Court Fudges Nuclear Arms Ruling; No Ban" and "Hague Court Declines to Give Ruling."[4] The ICJ's official language was that "the threat or use of nuclear weapons would generally be contrary to the rules of international law applicable in armed conflict, and in particular, the principles and rules of humanitarian law. However, in view of the current state of international law, and of the elements of fact at its disposal, the Court cannot conclude definitively whether the threat or use of nuclear weapons would be lawful or unlawful in an extreme circumstance of self-defence."[5] By the judges' own accounts, the language of the court's opinion was, at best, unclear.

The choice the court had made was not an easy one, and the court had struggled with the very nature of its answer.[6] Were the judges to determine whether or not the use of nuclear weapons was permitted by international law or prohibited? The judgment took the latter approach and determined that the threat or use of nuclear weapons was not impermissible under international law, a determination that made it possible for a nation to argue that its use of nuclear force was warranted and not illegal. Fifteen judges had to reach their decision applying the relevant facts to the applicable international law. The court heard oral arguments from representatives from twenty-two nations, including Takashi Hiraoka, Mayor of Hiroshima, and Iccho Itoh, Mayor of Nagasaki.[7] Other nations and civil society groups provided written arguments.[8] Russia, the United Kingdom, and the United States argued strongly that the legality of nuclear weapons depended on the circumstances of their use. Under international law, for example, self-defense was permissible, but aggression was not.

A closer look reveals the concerns and struggles each judge faced, as shared in the five declarations, three separate opinions, and six dissenting opinions of the judges.[9] Many judges expressed concerns that the court's opinion was not responsive to the question before it or went beyond what was being asked.[10] There was concern about the political context that led to the request for an advisory opinion and the potential for politicization.[11] In spite of the strong arguments by the United Kingdom and the United States that nuclear weapons were not prohibited by international law, the judges from those countries – Rosalyn Higgins and Stephen Schwebel – voted against the court's ruling. In her dissent, Higgins finds the court's ruling unconvincing on several grounds, noting in particular the unanswered question of "what military necessity is so great that the sort of suffering that would be inflicted on military personnel by the use of nuclear weapons would ever be justified?"[12] Schwebel, noting the "titanic tension between State practice and legal principle," states that, in this case, it is "more important not to confuse the international law we have with the international law we need."[13] In the end, every one of the fourteen judges wrote a declaration, separate opinion, or dissenting opinion explaining their views.[14] (One judge had died during the course of the proceedings, taking the court from fifteen judges to fourteen.)

Ultimately, the court's decision was split 7–7.[15] This meant that then ICJ President and Judge Mohammed Bedjaoui's vote would determine the outcome.[16] Bedjaoui decided that the court could not, on the basis of international law, determine the legality of the use of nuclear weapons by a state.[17] Today, nations continue to pursue, acquire and maintain nuclear weapons. China, France, Russia, the United Kingdom, and the United States all have nuclear arsenals. India, Pakistan, and North Korea claim to have them as well. This unprecedented moment in international law called on the woman and men of the court to decide a question paramount to the very survival of the planet. Their choice was legal. It was political. It was, in many respects, personal to every single being on Earth.[18]

Just fifty years earlier, most people could not imagine that such a magnificently tragic weapon could exist. That all changed in 1945. As US Secretary of War Henry Stimson described matter-of-factly in his diary: "[O]n August 6 a B-29 dropped a single atomic bomb on Hiroshima. Three days later a second bomb was dropped on Nagasaki and the war was over."[19] Within seconds, the bombs killed hundreds of thousands.[20] Within days, many more endured death by radiation.[21] Within weeks, Japan surrendered, bringing an end to the Second World War.[22] It was horrors like these that the ICJ was being asked to prevent by ruling that the use of nuclear weapons was not permissible under international law. The ICJ's ruling did not satisfy this request.

Let us return to how the existence of such a horrific weapon came to be in the first place. An abbreviated history starts in 1938 when German chemists Otto Hahn and Fritz Strassmann discovered nuclear fission, making the atomic bomb possible. The following year, scientists Otto Frisch and Rudolf Peierls determined how to operationalize uranium-235, the central element required to build the bomb. That same year, Albert Einstein (who had fled

Nazi Germany and emigrated to the United States in 1933) and Enrico Fermi (inventor of the nuclear reactor, who had fled fascist Italy) urged President Franklin Delano Roosevelt to develop an atomic bomb before Nazi Germany could do so.

President Roosevelt heeded the scientists' call and created a working group, known as the Manhattan Project. Two years later, in 1941, Roosevelt approved the atomic weapons program and established the Top Policy Group to provide oversight.[23] The group was originally composed of six members: Roosevelt (who reportedly never attended a meeting), Vice President Henry A. Wallace, Stimson, Chief of Staff of the Army General George C. Marshall, Office of Scientific Research and Development head Vannevar Bush, and chemist James B. Conant. Roosevelt decided to give the lead to the US Army instead of the Navy given the former's experience with large-scale construction projects. Secrecy was tight, although Roosevelt was known to have communicated with Winston Churchill about the possibility of atomic weapons.

After Roosevelt's untimely death on April 13, 1945, Harry S. Truman became the president who would oversee the end of the war. President Truman faced the grave choice of whether or not to use the atomic bomb and, in May 1945, created a secret high-level group known as the Interim Committee to advise him on the matter. It first met on May 9, 1945, and included three members of the original Top Policy Group: Stimson (acting as chair), Bush, and Conant. Wallace was out. New members included Secretary of State James Byrnes, Under Secretary of the Navy Ralph Bard, Assistant Secretary of State William Clayton, MIT President Karl Compton, and President of New York Life Insurance Company, George Harrison. Together, the group was tasked with advising the president on wartime controls and postwar policies related to nuclear energy.

On June 1, the Interim Committee came to a fateful decision:

> Mr. Byrnes recommended, and the Committee agreed, that the Secretary of War should be advised that, while recognizing that the final selection of the target was essentially a military decision, the present view of the Committee was that the bomb should be used against Japan as soon as possible; that it be used on a war plant surrounded by workers' homes; and that it be used without prior warning.[24]

The Interim Committee then consulted the Scientific Panel, comprising four physicists working on the Manhattan Project, including J. Robert Oppenheimer, director of the Los Alamos bomb assembly program. The panel agreed with the committee's decision that use of the bomb was warranted.[25] On receiving the panel's report on June 21, the Interim Committee finalized its position "that the weapon be used against Japan at the earliest opportunity, that it be used without warning, and that it be used on a dual target, namely, a military installation or war plant surrounded by or adjacent to homes or other buildings most susceptible to damage."[26] Three weeks later, the world's first atomic bomb explosion took place at the Trinity test site in New Mexico. On witnessing it, Oppenheimer channeled the *Bhagavad Gita*: "Now I am become Death, the destroyer of worlds."[27]

The United States had successfully detonated an atomic bomb. The next task became identifying its first target. To that end, ten members of the Target Committee, including General Groves, convened for the first time on April 27, 1945, in a conference room at 8:40 am where they determined the need for one primary and two alternate targets.[28] Consisting of military officials and scientists, the Target Committee went on to identify a list of Japanese cities to bomb based on geography, urban layout, population, strategic importance, and other military and scientific factors.[29] The aim was clear – use the bomb in a large city where the blast damage would kill many civilians. There were people making choices who viewed the people of Japan as subhuman, using the derogatory term "Jap" in the memos.[30] Thus, the decision about whether and where to use the world's first atomic bomb was influenced by these personal and often discriminatory views about the Japanese people alongside geopolitical and diplomatic considerations about how to end the war and secure the postwar world order.[31]

Ultimately, the target list of April 28, 1945, named seventeen cities and, in handwritten notes, showed Hiroshima, Kyoto, and Yokhama in order of preference.[32] Secretary Stimson did not like this list and ordered that Kyoto be removed.[33] (Niigata, Kokura, and Nagasaki were added later.)[34] In late July, General Leslie Groves sought to put Kyoto back on the list, arguing that it was a "first choice" for a target.[35]

It is here we see an intervention that would change the course of history. In spite of his support for using the bomb, Secretary Stimpson fought back to save Kyoto. He demanded that it be removed from the list of targets. Historians have analyzed why.[36] Kyoto was the traditional center of Japan and, in Stimson's view, destroying it might go too far, demonstrating a level of brutality that could frustrate postwar relations.[37] Stimson also had personal experience with Kyoto. He travelled there with his wife in 1926 and recalled with fondness its ancient shrines. We cannot know all that went into Stimson's choice to save Kyoto. But we do know how the story turned out. When General Henry Arnold sent the final target list to the

HEADQUARTERS ARMY AIR FORCES
TOP SECRET

ROUTING AND RECORD SHEET

By author
C.O., Iron Air Force

TALLY NO.
FILE NO.

7 Apr 1945

SUBJECT: Target Information

TO: Director, Joint Target Group

FROM: Chief of Staff, Twentieth Air Force

DECLASSIFIED
E.O. 11652,
NND 730039
By ERC NARS 06-4-74

DATE 28 Apr 1945

COMMENT NO. 1
RLS/mc/1h 72993

1. In connection with contemplated operations using high explosive "tall boy" (12,000 lb.) bombs detonated above the ground (about 200 feet altitude), it is requested that this Headquarters be furnished suitable target information of targets having the following specifications:

  a. They should be located in a reasonably large urban area but the target itself should not be less than three miles in diameter.

  b. They should lie on the Japanese main island area between Tokyo and Nagasaki.

  c. They should possess high strategic value.

2. The following are suggested as possible appropriate areas:

  a. Tokyo Bay
  b. Kawasaki
  c. Yokohama
  d. Nagoya
  e. Osaka
  f. Kobe
  g. Kyoto
  h. Hiroshima
  i. Kure
  j. Yamata
  k. Kokura
  l. Shimosenka
  m. Yamaguchi
  n. Kumamoto
  o. Fukuoka
  p. Nagasaki
  q. Sasebo

3. The destruction will primarily be accomplished by the air blast effect and the selection should be made with this thought in mind.

4. It will be appreciated if this information can be furnished to this Headquarters by no later than Saturday 5 May.

DECLASSIFIED
Authority NND 730039
BY _____ NARS, Date _____

LAURIS NORSTAD
Brigadier General, U. S. Army
Chief of Staff

TOP SECRET

J-1109 A.F.

2.2A U.S. Army Air Force Top Secret Memo, April 28, 1945

B. It was the recommendation of those present at the meeting that the first four choices of targets for our weapon should be the following:

  a. Kyoto
  b. Hiroshima
  c. Yokohama
  d. Kokura Arsenal

2.2B Summary of the Target Meetings, May 10 and 11, 1945

president on July 22, Kyoto was not on the list. Stimson, and his sentiment, had won.

On July 25, 1945, Groves delivered a finalized list of targets in a directive to General Carl Spaatz, in charge of the US Strategic Air Force in the Pacific. On August 6, Colonel Paul Tibbets led the bombing of Hiroshima. Three days later, the US Air Force bombed Nagasaki. The bombing killed more civilians than military personnel and the results were nothing short of horrific. In a letter to US Senator Richard Russell, President Truman immediately regretted his choice, noting "[my] objective is to save as many American lives as possible but I also have a human feeling for the men and women of Japan."[38] Stimson, however, would later say "this deliberate, premeditated destruction was our least abhorrent choice."[39]

The choice to use an atomic bomb for the first time, however, set in motion a series of events that led to the end of the Second World War and the beginning of the modern international legal system.[40] Just under three months after the bombs fell, on October 24, 1945, some fifty nations signed the United Nations Charter in San Francisco, giving birth to the United Nations and, with it, new rules and new institutions that have shaped our world ever since.[41] The use of the atomic bomb in 1945 would haunt the United Nations for decades and be cause for the ICJ's advisory opinion in 1996. In ICJ President Bedjaoui's own haunting words:

> "[W]ith nuclear weapons, humanity is living on a kind of suspended sentence. For half a century now these terrifying weapons of mass destruction have formed part of the *human condition*. Nuclear weapons have entered into all calculations, all scenarios, all plans. Since Hiroshima, on the morning of 6 August 1945, fear has gradually become man's first nature. His life on earth has taken on the aspect of what the Koran calls 'a long nocturnal journey,' like a nightmare whose end he cannot yet foresee."[42]

Bedjaoui's words ring true today for in this 'long nocturnal journey of war,' nuclear weapons, and international law, we see one constant – ourselves. At every turn, people make the choices that create or destroy our world. Therein, certain people make the choices that make or shape international law. Some choices matter more than others. Some choices change the world. Some choices can never be undone.

HOW INTERNATIONAL LAW UNDERSTANDS HUMAN CHOICE

Human choice is an inherent attribute of international law. How, then, does the field of international law currently understand choice? This chapter takes up that question and reviews the ways and means that international law currently uses to approach the study of choice, inclusive of decision making, judgment, and more. There is much to cover. Before doing so, I offer two initial perspectives. First, my assertion that human choice is integral to international law is a descriptive one. I leave aside, for now, normative questions about whether or not it should be. Second, this chapter is selective in its consideration of the vast literature in and around international law that deals with aspects of human choice. I do not engage certain theoretical aspects of international law and international relations centered around questions about state behavior or international organizational behavior as the focus here is on understanding human behavior. I acknowledge that there are many fascinating contributions from international legal theory and legal theory that may be relevant to the themes in this book and that, therefore, are ripe for future engagement.[43] I also see great potential for rich and vital dialogues in critical legal scholarship, including Critical Race Theory, Feminist Theory, Third-World Approaches to International Law (TWAIL), and LGBTQ+ theory, that can inform and be informed by a human choice approach to international law.[44]

One area of legal scholarship highly relevant to the study of human choice is legal process theory and international legal process theory. Legal process theory is an approach to law that originated with Henry M. Hart and Albert M. Sacks, who pioneered the American Legal Process School of legal theory in the 1950s. They proposed that public law is rooted in law's purposiveness, the coordination of institutions, and the legitimizing role of procedure.[45] This school emphasized the "centrality of process" in determining what law is and what it ought to be.[46] Hart and Sacks' work influenced and was influenced by the New Haven School, where Myres McDougal, Harold Lasswell, and Michael Reisman argued that "the most viable conception of law . . . [is] that of a process of authoritative decision by which the members of a community clarify and secure their common interests."[47]

In the 1960s, Abram Chayes, Thomas Erlich, and Andreas Lowenfeld introduced International Legal Process (ILP) theory, arguing that "[l]aw is rooted in shared values and shared purposes."[48] ILP examines the extent to which international legal processes influence decision making in international affairs, asking, for example, "[h]ow and how far do law, lawyers and legal institutions operate to affect the course of international affairs?"[49] Abram and Antonia Chayes later introduced the concept of managerial ILP, arguing that compliance with international law should focus on cooperation, capacity building, and problem solving.[50] Harold Koh extended ILP by considering the transnational dimension of interplay between domestic actors and nations.[51] These and subsequent ILP theorists argued that process matters in international law because it creates and changes norms.[52] New International Legal Process theory seeks to understand the relationship between legal process and normative purpose and envisions that decision makers will assume their roles in a timely manner.[53] It reflects the range of values "still to be distilled from many different participants in the international community and will thus make new law."[54] These approaches motivate us to think critically about who makes law and how law is made.

To answer questions like this, we can look to research on human behavior, choice, and decision making from a variety of fields.[55] First are theories developed in the field of traditional economics. Economic theory, broadly speaking, has long been based on the general premise that people choose the best option that is accessible or otherwise available.[56] In the 1950s, theories about such rationality led to early studies in decision theory on how agents make decisions and whether those outcomes are rational or optimal. These studies often used statistical or economic analysis.[57] As Rex Brown explains: "[T]he goal of [decision analysis] is comprehensive rationality – resolving the myriad of inconsistencies [sic] relevant to the choice in the decider's head – rather than just the limited coherence of a single model."[58] A form of decision theory, game theory, has long informed thinking about decision making in international relations leading to theories about "groupthink" and decision making in groups.[59]

Traditional economic theory also led to the development of rational-choice theory, which has significantly influenced legal thought about human choice. Developed in the 1980s, rational-choice theory, as described by Robert Keohane, is "based on the assumption of rationality."[60] Rational-choice theory argues that a person maximizes utility, or, simply put, does what he prefers.[61] It has caused debate and discord in international legal thought; its application in international law has been both lauded and criticized. Keohane, for example, states that "the field of international law has been quite resistant to rational choice analysis."[62] Keohane views rational-choice theory as an analytical tool that offers hypotheses but not conclusions. In international relations, he believes "that political actors behave strategically" most, if not all, of the time. Rational-choice theory has been used by scholars to understand the behavior of international institutions and international tribunals.[63] Herein, scholars have analyzed what motivates decision makers or agents, considering the influence of interests and values.[64]

Another approach to understanding human choice in law is found by scholars who employ behavioral science perspectives that challenge rational-choice theory and related core assumptions about rationality.[65] Starting with their seminal book, *Prospect Theory* (1979), psychologists Daniel Kahneman and Amos Tversky teamed up to show why assumptions about rationality in human choice are deeply flawed.[66] One branch of behavioral science, behavioral economics, seeks to acknowledge that traditional economic theory is built on assumptions that are sometimes inaccurate.[67] Scholars have problematized existing notions that rational-choice theory provides an accurate descriptive model of human behavior, as new research observes that people make choices that are not rational, often in predictable ways.[68] Consider, for example, cognitive biases that describe myriad ways in which our brains operate that cannot be classified as rational. Examples include positive illusions, when people are primed to be systematically biased in positive ways;[69] overconfidence, or overestimating one's knowledge;[70] illusory correlation, when one sees a relationship between two things that does not really exist;[71] and status quo bias, when we tend to prefer an option framed as the status quo.[72] Many biases relate to ways in which people interact with information. A bias known as anchoring, for example, shows up as the tendency to rely too heavily on the first information presented when making a decision.[73]

Heuristics, which are cognitive strategies or mental shortcuts we use in the face of complex or incomplete information to make decision making easier, also deviate from rationality.[74] Stereotyping, for example, evolved to enable us to process information quickly, even though our determinations based on stereotypes are often inaccurate and deeply flawed. Herbert Simon introduced the term "satisficing" to describe the ways our minds process judgments that are "good enough."[75] His insight was that, although rational people intend to be rational, we often lack the information necessary to make a rationally optimal choice.[76] Both cognitive biases and heuristics can inhibit optimum decision making and contribute to errors in judgment. People may also choose to avoid making any decision in uncertain circumstances.[77]

Behavioral approaches to international law, covering psychology, social science, economics, anthropology, and more, aim to investigate human behavior in international law.[78] Legal scholars are also employing empirical approaches, often with social-science methodologies, to study how legal actors think and decide.[79]

The theories, approaches, and methodologies above provide various ways to understand what international law is and how legal decisions in international law are made. They do not, however, speak to the human actor and the ways people form choices from a cognitive perspective. Returning to the ICJ's advisory opinion on nuclear weapons, we see why this matters. In speaking about his choice, ICJ President Bedjaoui said: "[N]ot for a moment did it fail to take into account this eminently crucial factor for the survival of mankind. The moral dilemma which confronted individual consciences finds many a reflection in this Opinion. But the Court could obviously not go beyond what the law says. It could not say what the law does not say."[80] In a similar vein, ICJ Judge Gilbert Guillaume shared his view of the court's opinion by stating that "it is not the role of the judge to take the place of the legislator. . . . It is the mark of the greatness of a judge to remain within his role in all humility, whatever religious, philosophical or moral debates he may conduct with himself."[81]

For all the theory and methods and approaches, judges and others often view international law as a set of positive rules that ought to be applied in a formalist way. But, as I have stated before, international law is more than rules.[82] International law involves the beliefs and values of those who shape it.[83] International law involves the understanding of legal decision making and other processes by which it is formed.[84] I am not alone in this view. Former ICJ President and Judge Higgins has rejected the idea of law as "merely the impartial application of rules," finding instead that "[i]nternational law is the entire decision-making process."[85] She argues that people who make decisions on the basis of international law, such as judges, legal advisors, and diplomats, do more than apply a rule; they also determine "what is the relevant rule."[86] Hersch Lauterpacht also believed that judges do more than find the rules; they "make choices."[87] Julius Stone proposes that we must study "the participants in the world power process."[88] All these people are onto something. In Chapter 3, we endeavor to discover what.

3

How People Choose

The first step to overturning conventional wisdom, when the conventional wisdom is wrong, is to look at the world around you.

Richard Thaler[1]

3.1 White matter fibers of the human brain, DSI scan. Credit: Alfred Pasieka/ Science Photo Library/Getty Images

How do people make choices? A short answer is that science is not absolutely sure. The longer answer is that science understands some, but not all, aspects of the complex cognitive activity in the human brain that produces what we might call a choice. To engage this complex area of study, the first question we might ask is what we mean by choice. I use the word *choice* in this book to describe the act or process of selecting or determining an outcome.[2] Choice is the activity we initiate in our brains to reach an outcome. This outcome can take various forms, such as a decision, judgment, assessment, or behavior.

Herein, choice is conceptually broader than decision making, which is trad-itionally understood as the process by which one reaches a decision.[3]

Our second line of inquiry concerns understanding how people make choices. In other words, how do people engage in choosing? We may use a variety of inputs. Some of these inputs come from the outside world, such as facts, evidence, or law. Some of these inputs come from within us, involving our experiences, emotions, values, or memories. If I asked you how you made a particular choice, what would you say? You might say you thought about it, did some research, weighed your options, or asked a friend for advice and then made up your mind. Your answer is accurate from your perspective. In the end, *you* made a choice. What, however, might you be missing? When we make choices, we remain largely unaware of the activity in our brain involved in choosing. We don't know which neural circuits we used or what areas of our brain were highly active. We are unaware of how our choices are influenced and even determined by our brains and the way they process memories, values, and emotions.

This brings us to the third element of understanding choice and the perspective that this chapter explores – understanding what happens inside our brains when we engage in choosing. Because the central aim of this book is to study human choice from a cognitive perspective, this chapter focuses on what leading research from neuroscience and related cognitive science tells us about the neurobiological basis of human choice, which can include biological, cog-nitive, developmental, social, and clinical aspects.[4] I use the term *neurosci-ence* broadly, recognizing that the field has an array of subspecialties such as cognitive neuroscience, social neuroscience, and affective neuroscience.

STUDYING HUMAN CHOICE

When we do something, think something, feel something, or say something, our brains are involved. We can think of the brain activity behind various actions as types of cognitive function. Perception, for example, involves seeing, hearing, tasting, smelling, and touching. Our brains process something our eyes see, and this activity can be associated with certain areas of the brain and also with circuits, or neural pathways, in our brain. In neuroscience, memory, emotion, attention, planning, setting goals, and switching tasks are classified as executive cognitive functions.[5] We might use several executive functions when we make a choice that results in a decision or a judgment; we may pay attention, gather information, make assessments about that informa-tion, plan ahead, recall a memory, and experience emotion. Consequently, the study of choice requires consideration of multiple areas of neurological research.[6]

Fortunately, new research from neuroscience and cognitive studies is beginning to reveal more about what our brains do when we make a choice. This research tells us new things and reaffirms old ideas, such as the propensity we have to make predictable choices that lead to outcomes we don't want.[7] Such insights show that human choice involves more than reason. It is more than thought. It involves a complex relationship among parts and circuits of our brain associated with emotion, empathy, bias, memory, and more.[8]

These many areas promise rich starting points for understanding human choice. As research focuses on the ways that biological data inform cognitive functions implicated in choice, choice increasingly is understood to be the function of the cognitive mechanisms that help a person differentiate between options. Certain topics, including trust, cooperation, uncertainty, reward, and loss, are considered theoretically relevant to the study of choice.[9] The study of emotion is vital to understanding human behavior because emotion can influence which areas of our brain are active, which in turn affects judgment and choice.[10] In addition, scientists have found that certain hormones stimulate certain functions. Oxytocin, for example, increases a person's sense of trust, which can result in strong feelings of affiliation with a group and lead, in turn, to altruism toward those in the group and an increased motivation to harm those who are not in the group.[11] Memory is another area of study in neuroscience with relevance to decision making.[12]

All this brings us to the important and complex question of research methodology. How do we know what we know? How do neuroscientists (and other researchers) study human choice? The methods used in cognitive research vary and can include animal studies, behavioral experiments on humans and computational modeling.[13] In neuroscience, brain imaging has become an important way to measure neural activity in different brain regions and networks and neural activity associated with different functions.[14] Noninvasive brain-imaging tools such as fMRI and PET scans, and newer techniques such as magnetoencephalography (MEG) scans can reveal what thousands of neurons in a person's brain are doing during any particular task or activity. As studies multiply, we continue to learn more about how a brain works during different types of cognitive activity. For example, memory and perception can be interrelated, with one influencing the other. A cautionary note is needed here. There is currently no grand theory or understanding of how the brain works as a whole, even though we know that it does.

The focus of this chapter is to highlight some of the central insights and ideas that have emerged from current neuroscience research relevant to the study of human choice. Neuroscientists who study human choice seek to understand what happens in the brain when a person deliberates and makes a choice. In simple terms, neuroscientific studies address "how" and "why" questions by showing the neural mechanisms responsible for an observed behavior. For example, we know that brain injuries can cause some people to have trouble making decisions. A 2005 study of forty-three people who survived head injuries engaging in a computerized betting game revealed that many of the subjects responded impulsively and made poor-quality decisions.[15] A later neuroscientific study employing fMRI imaging revealed that damage in the brain's orbitofrontal region "disrupted the ability to sustain the correct choice of stimulus ... and damage centered on dorsal anterior cingulate cortex led to the opposite deficit."[16] If proved accurate by future work, a study like this can help explain why and how an observed phenomenon occurs. Neuroscientific research has revealed, for example, that memory matters when people process choices about the future and that the hippocampus is engaged when processing memories.[17]

Of course, neuroscience is not the only field of study that offers valuable insights about human choice. There are many areas of important research across an array of fields and methodologies. Studies from various areas in psychology, such as experimental psychology, behavioral psychology, and behavioral economics, in which psychologists study economic choices, contribute to our understanding of human choice.[18] For example, researchers analyzing cognitive blindness have used controlled experiments on people to determine that distractions in our environment can cause us to perceive events inaccurately. This is illustrated by Christopher Chabris and Daniel Simons' now-famous video on the selective attention test demonstrating how many viewers watching a basketball game to count the number of passes fail to see the person dressed in a gorilla costume dancing across the screen.[19] International legal scholars have utilized such behavioral insights in various contexts.[20] There is also a wealth of research investigating how biases and heuristics shape our choices.[21] Earlier research on decision making from economics provided various theories, including the Rational Actor Model and the Expected Utility Model, that have been used in foreign policy decision analysis and game theory.[22] Overall, the research on decision making is abundant and this book does not attempt to include every area of research in its analysis. There are admittedly harder questions of how different areas of research salient to the study of human choice can and should intersect that are not taken up here.

This chapter presents information on what we currently know about human cognition associated with choice, recognizing that the research will continue to evolve. It focuses on areas of research relevant to the study of choice: thought, memory, empathy, emotion, and bias. Of course, this is not an exhaustive list, but it offers a good starting point for examining how people make choices. The unit of study is the individual and I make no claims about impacts on group decision making.[23] There is a growing body of information about what is possible and what brains can do; researchers have also made more general inferences about how most people's brains function even while recognizing variability, since each person's brain is unique. Some of this information is considered valid because it has been verified by many studies or enjoys widespread support by researchers. Other bits of information may be new or under question. Some of these insights are striking because they challenge or overturn earlier ideas; others are striking because they provide evidence for what may seem like common sense. It is worth noting that numerous concerns and questions about methodology exist both in and outside the field of neuroscience.[24] I refer eager readers to those best suited to respond to these questions, namely the researchers themselves.[25]

This chapter's central thesis is that understanding the neurobiology of the brain is crucial to understanding human choice, and understanding human choice is essential to understanding international law.[26] In recognizing that neurobiology underpins choice, we are led to analyze how factors we typically do not discuss in law, such as emotion or empathy, influence the choices of individuals empowered to shape international law. By deepening our know-ledge in this way, we gain a more accurate understanding of how choices in and about international law are made. This understanding, in turn, can better inform decisions about who should serve in these important decision-making roles. Diplomats, judges, and other elite decision makers in international law are not exempt from the cognitive biases and functions that affect us all, and learning about the processes of choice can empower and improve inter-national legal decision making.

HUMAN CHOICE AND THOUGHT

What is thought? Thought involves a complex array of variable brain activity associated with the higher level cognition involved in choice, executive function, judgment, and assessment. Nobel Prize-winning psychologist and economist Daniel Kahneman popularized the idea that our minds have two different thinking tracks in his book *Thinking Fast and Slow*.[27] In his view, the fast System 1 involves intuition, operates quickly and automatically, and is generally more resistant to change. The slower System 2, directed thought, is engaged when we concentrate and need to focus on complex choices.[28] This research helps disrupt old notions that the brain operates in a rigid left-side vs. right-side manner.[29]

There is no unitary process in the brain for thought.[30] Instead, our brains can employ a variety of areas and neural pathways when we think. We may draw on areas of the brain associated with emotion, memory, empathy, and bias. We know that certain locations in our brains become highly relevant for different types of cognitive activity. The prefrontal cortex, for example, plays a central role in how our brains synthesize information. A 2018 electrocortico-graphy study of sixteen people, in which electrodes were placed on the brain surface to measure the electronic activity of neurons, provides evidence that thought is organized in the prefrontal cortex.[31] This is just one study, and we cannot say that its findings, alone, are true or are the only truth. But similar findings could lead to a general inference that cognition associated with what we understand as thought is highly complex and involves the synthesis of various cognitive and neural inputs. Thinking involves more than reason or logic.[32]

A second insight relevant here is that thinking can occur in stages. For example, one fMRI study in which participants were trying to solve a math problem identified four stages of cognitive processes, categorized as encoding, planning, solving, and responding.[33] But a brain that is assessing information and thinking about the validity of facts in a legal case might engage in a different order of cognitive processes. The point is that our brains can invoke distinct centers and pathways that may differ depending on whether we are trying to assess information or solve a problem. Thought is not a one-size-fits-all endeavor.

Furthermore, our brains can engage in different kinds of thought. Goal-directed thought, for example, often occurs when we have the explicit aim of achieving a goal.[34] We try to focus on the objective and stay on task; this focus produces goal-directed thought, which utilizes our prefrontal cortex and enables it to focus attention on relevant stimuli and screen out irrelevant stimuli. This process is called cognitive control.[35] In a crude sense, focusing on making a decision helps our brains reduce the influence of distracting stimuli.

Deliberations, or thinking associated with decisions between various choices, can take more time, because our brains are relying on an accumulation of prior experiences, memories, and other evidence to inform a current choice. One brain-imaging study provided evidence that in choices involving decisions about what we value, the hippocampus, which has a part in process-ing memories, plays a key role in deliberating.[36]

Spontaneous thought, such as when our thoughts drift before we go to sleep, occurs when we are not engaging in attention-demanding activities.[37] Once possible benefit for such defocused thought may be that it allows our brains to maximize memory consolidation and access long-term memories.[38]

Thought associated with creativity involves cognitive activity in the prefrontal cortex and memory networks.[39] Herein, there is much to learn. For example, a 2005 study found that people solved anagrams more quickly when they were lying down than when they were standing up.[40] In another study, from 2002, people who were awakened from REM sleep were better able to solve anagrams than those awakened from non-REM sleep.[41] Currently, there is enough evidence to suggest that creative problem solving and goal-directed decision making recruit different brain processes and regions. Recognizing different types of thought from a neurological perspective allows for a deeper appreciation of how memory, emotion, motivation, and other factors work in complex ways to inform our thinking.

HUMAN CHOICE AND MEMORY

Memory describes the brain's capacity to retain, store, organize, and recall information over time.[42] Our past experiences and our memory of them can influence the choices we make today. In other words, prior experience guides present choices. The difficult questions to answer are why this is so and how it happens. Several areas of research inform the answers to these questions.

A 2017 study provided evidence that, under certain conditions, people make decisions about what to do by remembering similar choices they made in the past and whether those choices were successful.[43] For example, if you are trying to decide where to eat dinner, you might remember going to an Italian restaurant a month ago and having a nice experience or getting fast food and having an upset stomach. This study indicates that we pick relevant memories to inform current decisions, and consequently such memories would influence whether we choose fast food or Italian. They would likely have less influence if our decision was to try a new kind of food for which we have no memories or experience of.

HUMAN CHOICE AND EMPATHY

Empathy, the process by which a person infers the state of another person by generating a sense of that state in herself, is a cognitive skill essential for prosocial behavior.[44] However, the term *empathy* describes many responses, not just one. It identifies related but distinct phenomena of cognitive capacities and behavior that occur when a person responds with "sensitive care" to another's suffering.[45] One may come to know what someone else is feeling internally, feel what he or she feels, and/or match another's neural responses.[46] Evolutionary biologists have shown that this cognitive capacity developed in our species over millions of years.[47]

In the field of neuroscience, empathy research has taken off significantly in the last decade, and this research is shedding new light on old ideas. For example, it shows an apparent distinction between empathy and personal distress at the neurological level.[48] In other words, our brains process the pain we see another person experiencing quite differently from the pain we undergo ourselves. An important recent study also has shown that empathy is a cognitive skill that requires deliberation; it is not an automatic or inherent reaction.[49] One potential implication of this is that empathy may be something that must be taught, a skill acquired by learning.

Advances in brain mapping have led to the ability to map the "physiological correlates of the process of empathy, describe its neuronal architecture and specify empathy circuits in the brain."[50] Neural circuits are linked to our cognitive capacity for empathy.[51] For example, canonical neurons seem to link our perception with action.[52] The centers of neural activity involved include the right inferior parietal lobe (which processes the capacity to identify with others) and the anterior cingulate cortex, insula, thalamus, and somatosensory cortices (which process emotion).[53]

Pioneering work on mirror neurons by Marco Iacoboni, a professor of psychiatry and biobehavioral sciences at UCLA, reveals the science behind how people experience empathy and connection.[54] When our mirror neurons fire, our brain activates different areas depending on whether we take a first-person or a third-person perspective.[55] But mirror neurons may work differently in each individual.

Additional research has linked factors such as age and race to changes in how neurons function.[56] There is also neurological evidence that individuals differ in their capacity for empathy.[57] However, the study of empathy and cognition has led to widespread recognition in social psychology, sociology, and neuroscience of the phenomenon of emotional contagion, which occurs when people actually "catch" each other's feelings.[58]

Other studies are tracking two separate but connected processes involving empathy. The first process, sharing, occurs when you experience another's pain; sharing may produce an array of emotional responses ranging from empathy to disengagement.[59] The second process, mentalizing, occurs when, after reflecting on another's pain, one chooses an empathetic response.[60] These processes lead us to think of the cognition of empathy as a system of flexible representations that translate thought into feelings.[61]

How does empathy, as variously defined, play a role in choice? Although the question is straightforward, the answer is not. Psychologists have sought to understand the link through behavioral studies. One study showed that parents who more frequently reported feeling distress in response to a crying infant instead of feeling sympathy or compassion had a high risk of abusing a child.[62] Another study found that husbands who abused their wives had a significantly lower capacity for what is called empathy accuracy, or the ability to read other people's feelings and thoughts accurately.[63] A third study on emotional contagion indicated that what you feel is influenced by nonverbal cues of those around you, whereas what you think others are feeling is heavily influenced by what they have said.[64]

Although the study of empathy remains ongoing, two early implications emerge. First, the cognitive processes and brain structures used in empathy are also invoked during different kinds of decision making.[65] This suggests the potential for empathy and choice to interact at the cognition level. Second, it is probable that empathy is learned, not innate.[66] Such findings, if confirmed, should disrupt assumptions that people are born with, or lack, the capacity for empathy.

HUMAN CHOICE AND EMOTION

Emotion plays an important role in human choice and decision making.[67] Our neural activity and the neural systems that process choice can be connected to and intersect with neural systems that process emotion.[68] Explaining why this is so and how we know this is the case is more complex.[69]

Research by neuroscientist and professor António Damásio put forth neurobiological evidence for the notion that people make judgments not only by evaluating consequences and their probability, but also, and sometimes primarily, at an emotional level.[70] The foundational study underpinning this hypothesis found that patients with normal intellect who suffered trauma to their frontal lobes demonstrated abnormalities in emotion and feeling as well as in decision making.[71] Patients often decided against their self-interests and were unable to learn from previous mistakes.[72] The study concluded that such patients had mostly intact neuropsychological tests but were compromised in their ability to express emotion and feeling.[73] Without functioning emotional signals, a person had to rely on cost-benefit analysis for choosing between conflicting choices, which takes the brain more time to do.[74] Although some of Damasio's findings have been criticized, his research remains a leading source of support for the notion that emotion influences decision making, even if we remain unclear about how it does so.[75]

But do emotions *guide* decisions? Some research suggests that they can, sometimes. One study suggests that shutting down one's emotions can impair decision making.[76] A subsequent group of studies suggest that decision making is guided by emotional signals that are generated in anticipation of future events,[77] while an additional study found that people do not need to be aware of their emotions for this impact to occur.[78] These findings suggest that decision makers are affected by their emotional state even when they are not aware of the emotions they are experiencing.

One of the most studied emotions in connection with decision making is fear, which plays an important role in human cognition.[79] Imagine that you are afraid of snakes. When you encounter a real snake, your brain processes this in the amygdala. But if you worry about encountering a snake or see an image of a snake in a movie, your brain processes this in your ventromedial prefrontal cortex,[80] which couples knowledge about what something will feel like with real experiences.[81] The amygdala triggers emotions from an actual cause of fear,[82] such as seeing something that appears to be a snake moving through tall grass.[83] If someone's amygdala is not functioning properly, the connection between associations of loss and choice development becomes disrupted. As a result, a person may fail to avoid behaviors that lead to repeated negative emotions, such as losing money at a casino. If a person has an underlying neurobiological abnormality, they are likely to have behaviors that demonstrate repeated and persistent failure to learn from previous mistakes.

Another fMRI study revealed that when a brain faces a conflict between a belief and logic, it may change its reasoning process and recruit the right prefrontal cortex, which affords emotions – notably anger, fear, and empathy – a stronger role in decision making.[84] Fear can also stimulate more careful deliberative processes than normal because it links decision making with our working memory and emotion systems.[85] Research on how emotion may disrupt or enhance access to memory could have important implications for judicial behavior or national security decision making.[86]

Neuroscience demonstrates that our brains engage in a complex interplay of functions when we make a choice or a decision, and that emotion is a component of this. Yet people often want to know if emotions are "bad" for decision making. There is no single answer to the question. Context matters. It's true that the brain often experiences conflict between activating its emotion-processing networks and activating its reasoning-processing networks.[87] This helps to explain why people experiencing strong emotion – anger or joy – make different choices than they would make when calm. But the oft-repeated notion that wise decisions are made with cool (unemotional) heads is inaccurate. The somatic marker hypothesis explores how emotion can be integral to a particular decision-making task.[88] Emotion that is related to what you are deciding can benefit your decision-making cognition, while emotion that is unrelated can become a distraction.[89] Imagine you are driving a car on the highway and you have to decide whether or not to speed to make it to your final exam. The "thought" of being late or getting in an accident will evoke an emotional response (likely fear) that is related to your decision making and thus may be beneficial to your decision-making process. However, experiencing an unrelated emotion at this time, such as sadness at a loved one's death, may impede your decision-making process regarding speeding. This distinction does not always hold. Sometimes, related emotions can be disruptive, too.[90] The central lesson from this emergent emotion research is that attempts to study human decision-making behavior must take into account the impact that emotion can have on cognition. Ignoring emotion ignores the evidence.

HUMAN CHOICE AND BIAS

Aspects of our higher cognition include the mental activity we engage in when we formulate decisions, assess information, and make judgments. Various regions of our brain, and the neural circuitry that connects them, engage one another when we make a choice or change our mind.[91] Generally speaking, this is the reason why our biases can influence our cognition at the neural level. When we meet a stranger, for example, we immediately decide whether or not we think that person is a threat. In making such a choice, our brain may invoke past experiences, memories, and emotions, all of which shape our biases, and it may do this on a conscious level, leading us to have an explicit bias, or on an unconscious level, forming an implicit bias.[92] Thus, our choices and actions are influenced by factors we may be aware of or by "[h] idden internal events."[93] Understanding human choice this way helps us acknowledge the full array of influences that shape such choice.[94]

I use the term *bias* to describe a person's preference for, or aversion to, another person on the basis of their identity, which factors might include age, gender, or race. Many studies have confirmed that bias is real, and research investigating racial bias and neural activity confirms a link between what we think about a person and how our brains function.[95] Studies on racial bias show neural activity in the amygdala, which is also associated with fear.[96] For example, a 2014 review of neuroimaging studies investigating the "neural correlates of prejudice" argues that activity in the amygdala may be attributed to a person who perceives a threat that arises from negative cultural associations with black men and other groups.[97] Related to this work is the study of neural activity associated with in-group and out-group behavior.[98] Here, race, sex, gender, age, and other attributes all become factors in how we perceive and evaluate a person. When a person's identity is linked to a group other than ours, and this group has historically or culturally been associated with negative traits, we process such perceptions and biases in our amygdala, which is where we also process fear. Such insights into the neural mechanisms responsible for racial bias demonstrate that it is linked to fear, and while there are caveats and conditions to these findings, and future evidence will refine or extend earlier work, here neuroscience proves an essential tool for understanding and addressing bias.

CONCLUSION

Such evidence-based research gives us insight into our human brains and the connections between cognition and neural activity and the choices we make. This research also demonstrates the vast complexity involved in studying human beings. There are more questions than answers, and more gaps than certainties. This book fully acknowledges this reality. Instead of asking for final, certain answers from the continually evolving science and research, we must meet this topic with the curiosity and fluidity the study of human choice demands and deserves. We now know more than ever before about how humans think and choose, thanks to insights from neuroscience and related areas of study. In five years, we will know even more, affirming some ideas and updating others.

PART II

What does a more complete understanding of human choice mean for the study of international law? Part II of this book engages this question by journeying to some of the places where choices and decisions that shape international law are made. We will visit the grand halls of the International Court of Justice at the Peace Palace in The Hague and hear stories of the people who have served as judges there. We will consider tense decision moments at the round table of the United Nations Security Council in New York City. We will learn from the stories of those who have advanced human rights through the choices they made. This journey reveals certain perspectives. At the International Court of Justice, judges are expected to be of judicial temperament and not show emotion. At the United Nations Security Council, expressions of power are subject to far less scrutiny than expressions of compassion. In the realm of human rights, necessity and urgency often drive choices. These stories illustrate the many ways human choice shapes what international law is – and what it is not.

4

Human Choice at the International Court of Justice

There is in each of us a stream of tendency, whether you choose to call it philosophy or not, which gives coherence and direction to thought and action. Judges cannot escape that current any more than other mortals.

Benjamin N. Cardozo, former U.S. Supreme Court Justice[1]

4.1 Judges at the International Court of Justice convening to hear arguments in *Ukraine vs. Russian Federation*. Credit: Nacho Calonge/Contributor/Getty Images

The International Court of Justice (ICJ), established in 1945, is one of the most powerful institutions in the world. As the judicial arm of the United Nations, it interprets and shapes international law by adjudicating disputes between nations and providing advisory opinions.[2] Over the years, the court has settled numerous disputes over territory, boundaries, and treaty obligations and has provided advisory rulings on the biggest questions in international law.[3] In every case, the court's judgment is the result of choices made by the fifteen women and men serving on the court at that time. They hold the highest legal credentials and are carefully vetted and elected by both the UN General Assembly and the UN Security Council.[4] Collectively, these judges have the power to make decisions that bind nations.[5] Their rulings may be enforced by the UN Security Council.[6] In the international legal profession, there is no higher office.

Scholars have examined at length the ICJ's structure, purpose, and function.[7] The proliferation of international courts and tribunals in recent decades has led to renewed study of the ICJ, often in a comparative context.[8] International legal scholarship has focused on the court's institutional identity.[9] Similarly, in international relations, scholars generally study an international court as a single organizational entity that operates as an extension of state interests.[10] These important investigations tell us much about the ICJ as an institution and its impact on the world.

However, we know far less about how ICJ judges, as individual human beings, actually make the legally complex and often morally challenging choices they make.[11] Theories abound about how judges in a variety of legal contexts decide and what influences their decisions.[12] Perhaps the identity of judges, their education, and their expertise, matter.[13] It remains a possibility that national loyalties or concerns about professional reputation may sometimes influence judicial decision making.[14] Whether considering law's expressive function or factors such as political affiliation and bias, varied approaches offer ways to study judicial behavior.[15] But one finds little synthesis across these studies; divisions exist in the way we think about judges in national versus international courts, or in civil versus common law systems. In the end, we know that individuals serving as judges make the choices, judgments, and decisions that become the court's rulings. We just don't have a great grasp of how this happens.

This chapter begins the task of closing that knowledge gap. It describes the work of judges at the ICJ and the tensions between prevailing understandings of judicial choice and neuroscientific understandings of human choice, as examined in Chapter 3. It frames the ICJ not only as a monolithic institution but also as a living, breathing collection of individuals who make deliberate choices – choices influenced by thought, empathy, emotion, and bias. Each person who becomes a judge has internal cognitive processes for executive functions, judgment, and other processes associated with decision making. These processes and other features of cognition are affected by every judge's unique identity, life experiences, memories, and emotions, all of which inform choice. Deciding matters involving tragic and disturbing events naturally provokes more than reason or thought. Ultimately, judges' choices reflect that they, like all of us, are human, a reality that should be openly recognized and embraced.

DECIDING GENOCIDE

Genocide is wrong. When the government of Nazi Germany exterminated over six million Jewish people in the 1930s and 1940s, it was wrong.[16] When the Khmer Rouge killed roughly a fourth of the population of Cambodia in the late 1970s, it was wrong.[17] When Hutu-led forces in Rwanda took the lives of between 500,000 and 1.1 million people they believed to be Tutsi during a span of four months in 1994, it was wrong.[18] Mass graves piled high with unidentified bodies reveal little of the individual lives lost to murder and to madness.

Genocide is a deplorable horror. It is illegal everywhere.[19] Nations around the world, and their leaders, are on notice that genocide is an international crime, as codified in the Rome Statute and the Convention on the Prevention and Punishment of the Crime of Genocide (the Genocide Convention), and as a matter of international customary law.[20] Genocide is a *jus cogens*, a norm from which states cannot derogate. As a result, states have a duty to prohibit genocide and to prosecute those who commit it. For some, the gravity of the crime of genocide lies in the sheer magnitude of the loss of life. For others, it lies in the sordid purpose that drives the violent plans of the perpetrators. Such purpose – the specific intent to eliminate an entire category of people based on some aspect of their shared identity – defines genocide and distinguishes it from other crimes against humanity.[21] Yet in spite of its prohibition, genocide remains a problem that international courts and tribunals have been called on to address.[22] The ICJ is one of them.

Imagine that you are one of fifteen judges elected to the court. Imagine that you must exercise your judicial decision making on a case alleging genocide and that, like most people, you believe that genocide is not only illegal but also abhorrent. The only formal guidance you have concerning judicial judgment comes from Article 20 of the ICJ Statute, which requires you, and all members of the court, to take an oath to "exercise his powers impartially and conscientiously."[23] But before you can consider the merits of the case, you and your colleagues have to determine if the court has the requisite jurisdiction to take it up in the first place. Your training and professional expertise tell you to examine the facts in light of the applicable international law. Your colleagues at the court aim to do the same. In that sense, a case of alleged genocide is no different from any other case.

However, this case *is* different. It concerns alleged acts of genocide that are happening right now, even as you read the pleadings. Children are dying. People are relying on the court's protection. You think of the court's advisory opinion of 1951, when it wrote that genocide is "a crime under international law involving a denial of the right of existence of entire human groups, a denial which shocks the conscience of mankind and results in great losses to humanity, and which is contrary to moral law and to the spirit and aims of the United Nations. (Resolution 96 (1) of the General Assembly, December 11th 1946)."[24] You may feel conflicted. As a judge, your professional duty is to decide the case before you in an impartial manner. But as a human being, you cannot help being affected. Maybe you lose sleep at night. Maybe you think about what is happening so very far from the city in which you work, The Hague. Time passes and you must decide where you stand on the case. What choice will you make? How will you make it?

This was precisely the situation before the ICJ in May 2002, when the government of the Democratic Republic of Congo (DRC) brought an application against Rwanda. The application alleged that Rwanda had engaged in "massive, serious and flagrant" violations of human rights and international humanitarian law as a result of Rwanda's armed aggression against Congolese people in the territory of the DRC.[25] The DRC's claim of genocide had its roots in the Rwandan genocide of 1994, when a Hutu-led government in Rwanda targeted and slaughtered Tutsi, Twa, and moderate Hutu in Rwanda. In 2002, the Rwandan government (no longer Hutu-led), under the leadership of President Paul Kagame, engaged in controversial security operations in DRC territory against alleged Hutu loyalists who had fled Rwanda after the 1994 genocide.

The DRC put forward eleven legal grounds on which the ICJ could find it had jurisdiction. The Court's analysis of the jurisdictional issue focused generally on the nature of state reservations to treaties and specifically on Rwanda's reservation to the Genocide Convention. When Rwanda ratified the convention in 1975, it entered a reservation that it would not be bound to Article IX, which effectively provides that disputes arising out of the convention shall be submitted by state parties to the ICJ. The court first considered whether Rwanda's reservation was still valid.[26] After the 1994 Rwandan genocide, various state officials had made statements about Rwanda's commitment to preventing genocide and its intention to remove its reservation to the Genocide Convention. However, the court determined that the statements made by Rwandan officials regarding withdrawal did not take "international effect," as Rwanda had not notified other nations that were party to the convention, as required by Article 22 of the Vienna Convention on the Law of Treaties.[27] The

ICJ further determined that the presence of *jus cogens* and the creation of rights and obligations *erga omnes* embodied in the Genocide Convention did not, in and of themselves, create jurisdiction for the court to hear the case. The court decided that a reservation regarding dispute settlement was not incompatible with the object and purpose of the convention.[28] The court's February 3, 2006 judgment, authored by then ICJ President Shi Jiuyong, found that it did not have jurisdiction to entertain the DRC's application and that it was not required to rule on its admissibility.[29] The court's view was that its jurisdiction must be based on the consent of the parties and could not be found solely on the *jus cogens* nature of the issue in the case.[30]

The legal outcome was logical. International jurists agree that the ICJ cannot insert itself into legal matters where it lacks jurisdiction. To do so would go beyond its mandate pursuant to the UN Charter. But many thought the court's judgment, although legally tenable, was deeply unjust. As the DRC claimed in its pleadings, how could the court allow Rwanda to behave in such a contradictory fashion in rejecting the ICJ's jurisdiction when almost a decade earlier it had called on the UN Security Council to prosecute genocide against Rwandan people?[31] In the end, the court determined that even though genocide was a *jus cogens* or preemptory norm, that was not grounds to invalidate Rwanda's (or any state's) reservation to the Genocide Convention stating that it did not consent to the jurisdiction of the ICJ.[32]

A case like this highlights the need to understand the distinction between how a judge decides cases pursuant to the ICJ Statute, professional norms, and long-standing practice, and how a human being makes choices involving profound consequences. Of course, it is worth clarifying at the outset that we have no way of actually knowing how each judge reached her or his decision in this case. However, a close look at the court's judgment reveals further insights.

The court's judgment was 15–2.[33] Those in the majority were President Shi; Vice President Ranjeva; judges Vereshchetin, Higgins, Parra-Aranguren, Kooijmans, Rezek, Al-Khasawneh, Buergenthal, Elaraby, Owada, Simma, Tomka, and Abraham; and Judge ad hoc Dugard. Those in the minority were Judge Koroma and Judge ad hoc Mavungu. Despite the strong majority in this case, several judges wrote separate opinions further explaining their views. The separate opinion authored by judges Higgins, Kooijmans, Elaraby, Owada, and Simma, for example, sent a strong message about their discontent with the constraints on the court's jurisdiction:

> It is a matter for serious concern that at the beginning of the twenty-first century it is still for States to choose whether they consent to the Court adjudicating claims that they have committed genocide. It must be regarded as a very grave

matter that a State should be in a position to shield from international judicial scrutiny any claim that might be made against it concerning genocide. A State so doing shows the world scant confidence that it would never, ever, commit genocide, one of the greatest crimes known.[34]

Years later, Judge Simma, who coauthored this separate opinion, offered the following reflections:

"It was clear to me based on prior work I had done and insight I had gained in the International Law Commission, it was not possible [for the Court] to change course from the direction of the Court's 1999 decision in the Yugoslavia case. So the Court cannot say 'it is simply awful to discard making a decision about genocide' but we could write this opinion to say things have changed since 1951 and to steer the Court toward the future to signal that 1999 was not the last word. The five of us [authoring the separate opinion] were unhappy with the state of the law as the Court saw it. The goal of the Separate Opinion was to say we are unhappy with the state of the law on human rights as developed by the Court."[35]

This was also clearly communicated publicly by Judge Elaraby in his declaration stating that "[t]he Court's inability to examine the merits due to jurisdictional limitations cogently demonstrates a major weakness in the contemporary international legal system."[36]

Judge Koroma's dissenting opinion went further still. His legal analysis led him to find that Rwanda's reservation to Article IX did not prevent the court from inquiring into the state's responsibility for genocide. He offered the following strongly worded commentary:

The allegation involving the commission of genocide is far too serious a matter to be allowed to escape judicial scrutiny by means of a procedural device. The nature of the Convention and gravity of the allegation dictate that, wherever possible, it must be subject to judicial scrutiny. Inasmuch as Rwanda was able to call on the international community to hold to account those alleged to have committed genocide in Rwanda itself, it cannot justifiably shield itself from enquiry in respect of the very kinds of acts for which it succeeded in obtaining scrutiny by a competent organ. In other words, it is neither morally right nor just for a State to shield itself from judicial scrutiny under Article IX of the Convention in respect of acts alleged to have taken place in the territory of a *neighboring* State when those acts constitute the very same conduct as that in response to which the State successfully urged the establishment of an international tribunal for the prosecution of persons responsible for genocide and other serious violations of international humanitarian law.[37]

Together, these statements – both public and private – demonstrate that the judges' determination of the judgment in this case were produced by more than a formulaic application of law and fact. These statements show how the judges' perspectives, emotions, and beliefs about the nature of a crime dealing with genocide helped inform their decision making. Like all of us, judges bring human aspects to their judicial decision making. While they decided the case based on facts and international law, they were not immune to other factors.

In considering how cases may or may not impact one's stress level, Judge Simma notes that there are "two different reasons to lose sleep. One would be if you really fight with yourself or engage in a process about how to decide a case; that can cost you good sleep. The other would be that you have a view of the law and you know how you will decide but you are impressed by what you hear about the opposite side. In a difficult case, I don't lose sleep over the legal decision if I think it was correct. Where I did lose sleep was where we were shown a video where a paramilitary group had killed a number of young Bosniaks, and that left a lasting impression."[38]

This intimate chronicle, a rare glimpse into the experience of judging a case involving genocide, illustrates the human heart that beats behind judicial choice. It also opens the door for us to ask even more questions about the judicial decision-making process. What influence, if any, did the fact that the case concerned a matter as horrific as genocide have on the judges? What emotions surfaced? Did any judge empathize with the alleged Congolese victims? Did any of them empathize with Rwanda, given that many people there had suffered genocide just a decade earlier? Did some judges respond to graphic depictions of events in the DRC, such as the video, by numbing their emotions, while other judges accepted their feelings? Had any of the judges been to the DRC? Factors like these generally do not have a place in the traditional analysis of judicial decision making. However, such factors do matter in understanding human choice and human cognition.

UNDERSTANDING JUDICIAL CHOICE AS HUMAN CHOICE

Because the decisions taken, or not taken, by the International Court of Justice have the power to bind states, render justice, promote peace, and save lives, how the court reaches its judgments is a matter of great interest and importance. This book argues that we need to understand that the ICJ is more than simply an institution, and its role in shaping international law requires a deeper appreciation for the possibilities and limits of human choice. This is a conversation different in kind and scope about judicial behavior than scholars commonly have. From this perspective, the study of judicial choice is integrally linked to insights about human choice. We should not merely ask why the ICJ adopts particular views of the law. We should also consider how individual judges serving on the court reach the particular views they do.

One way of ascertaining how people make the choices they do when they are judges at the ICJ is to ask them. So that's what I did. I interviewed four ICJ judges who were willing to share some thoughts on their processes when determining a judicial opinion; I also spoke with several international arbitrators. I have the utmost respect for them and am grateful for their willingness to speak with me. I also have drawn from preexisting interviews and from what various judges have said in speeches, remarks, or their written opinions and judgments. This methodology is imperfect; I offer no claim that these stories represent anything more than illustration. Here is what I found.

To begin with the basics, judges may have different approaches to the facts themselves. Some judges will only consider facts presented before the court in the parties' pleadings. Judge Buergenthal explained: "I will not look at the news and I try to avoid the Internet as to avoid tainting my view with facts from the outside."[39] Others take a broader approach. Judge Simma recalls: "My approach to evidence in this case was to learn as much as I could about the topic. I had read a book about the war in Yugoslavia and was interested in knowing as much as possible. I think [the difference in approaches] has to do with the way judges and lawyers approach process in the civil law vs. common law systems. In the common law system, the facts are put before you. The facts that you are to consider are the ones people put before you and whoever does a better job in presenting the facts wins. The aim is not to discover objective truth. ... In civil law, it is different. For me it is impossible to limit my thinking to this adversarial mode. I automatically fall into inquisitorial.

I want to know what is true, what really happened and I will search for it, if necessary, by my own means. It is totally legitimate, even highly desirable for a person deciding whether genocide has happened to know as much as absolutely possible."[40]

These perspectives matter because they give context to the reality that each judge makes choices in different ways. People make choices in different ways. When we watch videos or listen to a podcast or read words on paper, our brains process each input in distinct ways.

Judges also differ in how they arrive at the decision to follow a majority opinion or to write their own. Judge Buergenthal, in speaking about his decision in the *DRC* v. *Rwanda* case, said: "I always felt that I would only write a separate opinion if there was a principle, a view I thought I had better put down. I didn't feel so in this case. The human element challenged my extraneous notions, not my juridical ones."[41] He went on to share with me how unfortunate it was for him to see Rwandans, who had suffered heavily, treat other people in such a way. Judge Buergenthal further notes: "[M]y long critique of the ICJ. We never engaged in juridical or policy making. Why not think about matters of human and political significance? Those issues never came out. They came out at the Inter-American Court."[42]

Should judges at the ICJ and elsewhere acknowledge and discuss the empathy, emotions and possible biases they have? From a human choice approach, emotion, empathy, bias, and other aspects of our human experience are a normal part of our cognitive processes associate with making choice. Yet, judges are expected (or expect themselves) to act otherwise. Judge Simma notes: "I don't recall having any conversations with other judges about how we felt in a case."[43] Judge Buergenthal recalls one time where a fellow judge expressed emotion to him and noted it was the exception, not the rule.[44] Georges Abi-Saab, in his wisdom, reflects that "[h]uman tragedy spurs you to find ways and means of making the law matter."[45]

These judges share their own reflections of their experiences serving on the ICJ. They give voice to the reality of human choice and human behavior that this book has explored. Such insights ask international law to consider, anew, how people serving as judges ought to acknowledge and engage their own emotions and more. Is it desirable for a judge to keep quiet about such things among colleagues? Do shows of emotion strengthen public trust in courts? Shouldn't judgments, as Judge Simma advises, be "morally valuable and intellectually digestible?"[46] If judges have emotions but just don't show them, is this what was intended by juridical adherence to impartiality?

Let's consider another tough case, brought by Paraguay against the United States in 1998. The United States imposed the death penalty against a Paraguayan man, Angel Francisco Breard, who was found guilty of raping and murdering a woman in Virginia. The court ordered the USA to halt actions to execute Breard due to its obligations under the Vienna Convention on Consular Relations.[47] In a separate declaration, Judge Oda noted that he disagreed on the legal reasoning but acknowledged he voted "in favour of the Order, for humanitarian reasons,"[48] a clear statement that something beyond impartial legal reasoning was at work in his decision to vote in favor of the order. The USA ignored the court's order and Breard was put to death by the state of Virginia that same year.

A few years later, in 2001, the court decided a similar case brought by Germany against the USA for violations of the same Vienna Convention. Two brothers, Karl-Heinz and Walter Bernhard LaGrand, were convicted of murder in Arizona and sentenced to death.[49] The court ruled that the USA had violated its treaty obligations on several fronts and, for the first time, established that provisional measures of the court are binding on nations.

Judge Oda dissented with the majority in this case on several grounds. But, to focus on the study of judicial choice in this chapter, let me point out what Judge Oda said about his decision.

Germany had sought provisional measures to prevent the USA from executing Walter LaGrand prior to the ICJ's final decision in the case. The ICJ granted such measures in its Order on Provisional Measures of March 3, 1999.[50] Judge Oda had agreed to the order but wrote a declaration explaining his "great hesitation" in doing so and emphasizing that he voted in favor of the order "solely for humanitarian reasons."[51] Judge Oda later reflected: "I now regret that I voted in favor of that Order since I did so against my judicial conscience," noting that he did so "to maintain the solidarity of the Court and out of humanitarian concerns."[52] This clear statement of the conflict a judge may feel between legal impartiality and an emotional or empathetic response to circumstances, or to institutional integrity, highlights Abi-Saab's observation that certain kinds of case raise different concerns and issues for judges. Judges may react differently to a case involving genocide than they do to a case involving the death penalty. Perhaps the link between such cases is a concern about humanitarian issues.[53]

Here we can plainly see the need to analyze judicial choice as human choice. These personal accounts of ICJ judges push us to acknowledge that each ICJ judge employs his or her own approach to judicial decision making. Judges should not be asked to deny their emotions, biases, feelings of empathy, or other realities involved in human choice. Given the research, it is questionable whether such a denial is, in fact, possible. Instead, judges should be able to acknowledge all of their human attributes in making decisions. Thus, taking up the relevant areas of research on human choice introduced in Chapter 3, lets us consider how insights about emotion, empathy, bias, and other factors may inform our understanding of judicial choice.

EMOTION

International judges ascribe to their role and purpose a commitment to work within the constraints of the law. The accepted understanding of judicial decision making is that the judge is to apply the applicable law to the facts presented before the court. A judge ought to do this impartially. Emotion does not play a starring role in this story. The prevailing assumption is that if a person has feelings this, somehow, gets in the way of reason and good judgment.

Leaving aside for a moment the all-important question of how we might define the concept of good judgment, let us consider the evidence introduced in

Chapter 3 regarding when and whether emotion influences reason and judgment.[54] Think about the last major choice you made. In your decision-making process, you may have considered the information you had, your prior experience, your hopes and fears, or other factors. But these were only the factors of which you were aware. Your brain accessed an array of sources, including past memories, emotions, biases, and more, during the cognitive activity that resulted in a choice, and it did this on an unconscious level. These aspects of your cognition are implicit, because they remain unknown to you, the decider.

Insights from neuroscientific research help us to understand that our choices are the result of a complex web of brain activity. Thus, when a person is called on to judge a legal case, one cannot restrict one's cognitive activity to unbiased legal reasoning alone or put aside one's emotion when applying the law to the facts. This isn't how the human brain works. Our cognitive activities associated with choice can be affected by our emotions even when we are unaware of them. Neural systems that process judgment and memory intersect with and also share neural systems that connect to the executive functioning associated with making choices. That's why emotion plays an important role in decision making.[55]

Emotion intersects with memory, judgment, and other cognitive functions in ways that are both beneficial and detrimental to decision making.[56] Recall the research in Chapter 3 showing that emotion may influence choice in ways deemed both good and bad. In addition, the brain often experiences conflict between activating its emotion-processing networks and activating its reasoning-processing networks. This helps to explain why people who are experiencing strong emotions of any sort make different choices than they would otherwise make. We cannot always choose to put our emotions aside; they influence us at the cognitive level even if we don't know that they are doing so. The broader point we need to recognize is that neuroscience helps explain the complex interplay of functions our brain engages in when making a choice or arriving at a decision. It is not possible for people to separate emotion from reason at the cognitive level, even when we think we can.[57]

What we know about how the brain actually works suggests that the prevailing story of judicial decision making does not hold. Of course judges should decide cases based on law, but because we know emotion will play a part in their decision making, they should be allowed to acknowledge that they have emotions about cases, especially when deciding matters of global historical importance and human impact.

Take the experience of former judge Georges Abi-Saab, who served at the International Criminal Tribunal for the Former Yugoslavia (ICTY). Abi-Saab describes his experience deciding *The Prosecutor v. Duško Tadic,*[58] in which Tadic was prosecuted for committing war crimes at a Serb-run concentration camp in Bosnia-Herzegovina during the Bosnian war:

> There, the feeling was very strong and emotional because there was a war going on, people being killed, massacred, and we were aware in the Tribunal of not being able to do much about it because of the limits to jurisdiction. Then this case came. Tadic was a small torturer in one of the camps. He happened to be taken in Munich because he had a brother who had a restaurant there. The Germans arrested him and they wanted to deliver him to us, but they didn't have the enabling legislation and had to adopt it and conclude an agreement with the Tribunal. It was not the most important case but it was something to be done, however small it was. Here we were not against a person but we wanted to put the machinery of justice to work. It was very tough but important to contain the enthusiasm so that we don't act as prosecutors but as judges. The feeling was emotionally charged both in public opinion and within the Tribunal against what was going on. But it was important to act as a Tribunal.[59]

This account by Abi-Saab once again reveals the reality that courts and judges are not immune to human experience.[60]

BIAS

Recall, again, from Chapter 3 that a bias is a tendency that can manifest as a preference for or an aversion to something or someone. From a cognitive perspective, these tendencies can create and reinforce neural pathways in the brain. When that happens, choice can be affected. If a tendency becomes habit, people can engage in heuristics, such as stereotyping, of which they are unaware. Our identity or how we perceive ourselves in relation to others influences bias in important and complex ways. Many people have a tendency to prefer and empathize more with people we believe to be like us. Judges at the ICJ, and elsewhere, aim to remain impartial in cases but they are not immune to this common human tendency to develop preferences for or aversions against people.[61] In other words, because human bias exists, judicial bias is always possible.

The question of judicial bias came up in the court's 2004 advisory opinion on the construction of a wall in the occupied Palestinian territory. The court found that Israel's construction of the wall and related activities were contrary to international law, as they breached the Palestinian people's right of self-determination.[62] The court strongly sought a unanimous decision in this case, given the political sensitivities surrounding the legal issues.[63] At the time, the court included Judge Shi as president and judges Koroma, Higgins, Kooijmans, Elaraby, Owada, Ranjeva, Guillaume, Vereshchetin, Parra-Aranguren, Rezek, Al-Khasawneh, Buergenthal, and Tomka. Only Judge Buergenthal voted against the court's order.

I sat down with Judge Buergenthal, who shared some of his reflections about the case. He declined to join the court's majority opinion on judicial ethics grounds. He believed that Judge Elaraby should have been disqualified from the case due to actual bias or the potential for bias.[64] Judge Buergenthal based his view on an interview Judge Elaraby gave in August 2001 to the *Al-Ahram Weekly* online newspaper on his views about Israel's occupation of Palestine.[65] Judge Elaraby spoke in his personal capacity; he was not in office and not yet elected to the ICJ. Based on the interview, in which Judge Elaraby appeared critical of Israel, the government of Israel requested that the ICJ disqualify Judge Elaraby from hearing the case, alleging that he was "actively engaged in opposition to Israel including on matters which go directly to aspects of the question now before the Court."[66] Article 17 of the ICJ Statute aims to reduce bias by a standard of judicial ethics mandating that no judge on the court may participate in a decision about a case in which he was previously involved (as counsel, agent, advocate, or member of another tribunal). Judge Buergenthal further stated that this discrete standard was intended to be taken broadly to ensure the judges of the court "operate in broader conceptions of justice and fairness" to "preserve their legitimacy."[67] Were Elaraby's on-the-record statements sufficient to show involvement in the issue that could result in bias? Did the court agree on the very meaning of what bias was and how to know if a judge has it? In this matter, the ICJ declined to disqualify Judge Elaraby.

Another account of judicial choice and bias described by Judge Simma dealt with the question of state immunity in cases of war crimes and crimes against humanity. One country had alleged that its neighboring country was responsible for acts amounting to such crimes within its territory. As the Judge Simma explained: "I cared about human rights. I was an international human rights lawyer. You find yourself in a special situation. There was a great expectation on the part of the human rights movement out there that the ICJ would be progressive and support that movement."[68] Judge Simma dealt with this dilemma by inserting the language "the last word is not spoken" into the opinion affirming state immunity.[69] He further recalled, "my conscience was not unaffected."[70] Speaking more broadly about judicial choice in international law, Abi-Saab remarks that "in cases where political opportunities override legal principles, there can be a lack of courage to tackle the real but tough issues and say the truth."[71]

Examples like these demonstrate the tensions that arise between the pre-vailing idea of judicial choice and the reality of being a human who brings their individual and professional selves to the job. As leading international arbitrator and professor Laurence Boisson de Chazournes advises: "[B]eing moved by events or a situation a judge or an arbitrator is facing does not mean that she is not impartial and will not remain impartial. She is a human person with her own emotions but she is also a professional."[72] This insight raises important questions about how we conceptualize impartiality taking account the neuroscientific realities of emotion, bias, and more. Should judges and arbitrators acknowledge emotion in their judicial choice? How ought people in these roles approach their implicit biases?

These stories illustrate a central inference from neuroscientific research in this area. All humans have the capacity for bias. Judges are not exempt. As ICJ Judge Joan Donoghue advises;

> "[t]he most important quality for deciding a case is self-reflection because nobody is truly neutral about anything. We bring to an issue whatever set of biases we have. One must question one's initial reactions. The ideal is to be constantly self-reflective and open to understanding the reasons for one's decisions."[73]

This book encourages us to be aware that such biases are real and to better understand why we have them.

TRUST

Emotion and bias are not the only aspects of human choice that may be relevant to the study of judicial choice. Many others are worthy of study and investiga-tion. For example, what role does trust between judges (or the lack of trust) have in persuasion? A judge may more likely to be persuaded by a fellow judge's position in a case if he trusts that judge. For one judge, trust rested on a sense that the fellow judge seemed objective.[74] Many adjudicators, judges, and arbitrators may share such experiences. For example, international arbitrator and professor Lucy Reed reflects: "[W]hen I observe genuine emotion from counsel, that increases their credibility to me."[75] In deciding what information she trusts as an arbitrator, Reed notes that reputation and expertise matter. Examples like these require us to consider why? If I find that trusting a person makes her more persuasive to me, why is that so from a neuroscientific perspec-tive? The answers (there are several) are longer than this chapter has space to engage in, but one study, for example, links the experience of trust to the production of oxytocin, the feel-good hormone, in the brain.[76] The general finding that oxytocin production is involved in an experience of trust has also been backed up by other neuroscientific studies.[77] Such research informs our understanding of choice by showing that trust is an important aspect of the judicial decision-making process.

WHY THIS MATTERS

Revisiting the Aristotelian view in the twenty-first century requires reexamining antiquated beliefs about judging and judges. The old story tells us that good judging ought to be devoid of emotion and that preserving the important judicial standard of impartiality requires not acknowledging one's feelings or bias. The current conventional view is that judges, being of high intellectual capacity and strong moral integrity, make choices by applying international law to the facts presented before the court.[78]

These views are outdated and incorrect. Humans simply don't work this way. And, in an effort to adhere to such views, our expectations of judges risk denying core aspects of their humanity. As US Supreme Court Justice Stephen Breyer reminds us:

> Law requires both a head and a heart. You need a good head to read all those words and figure out how they apply. But when you are representing human beings or deciding things that affect them, you need to understand, as best you can, the workings of human life, [and in hard cases] where perfectly good judges come to different conclusions on the meaning of the same words ... it is very important to imaginatively understand how other people live and how your decisions might affect them, so you can take that into account when you write.[79]

The new story is a human-choice approach for evaluating judicial decision making. Given all we have learned about human choice, significant evidence suggests that one does not choose through thought alone. To understand fully how judges make choices that affect their judicial decisions, we have to account for the evidence about how people make choices. Experience, identity, bias, and emotion (and other factors) play an important role in the cognitive processes involved in human choice.[80]

Developing such a human-choice approach requires interdisciplinary collaboration between the fields of study relevant to human behavior including neuroscience, cognitive studies, psychology, and genetics, in addition to law.[81] Some areas of legal scholarship have begun this enterprise.[82] As I see it, the purpose is to develop existing ideas about how judges decide through a human-choice lens. For example, any judge may have a policy preference, or be concerned with their reputation.[83] The human-choice model would evaluate how those aspects interact at the cognitive level when making choices.

As we look to the future, the need for a human-choice model becomes clear. The ICJ has recognized that its work is becoming increasingly challenging, in legal and extralegal ways. In its 2005–2006 annual report for that year, the court discussed how the cases before it are increasingly fact-intensive, requiring the court to carefully examine and weigh the evidence. The court stated "[n]o longer can it focus solely on legal questions"[84] and that it finds itself to be "seized by cases concerning more 'cutting-edge' issues, such as allegations of massive human rights violations, including genocide, the use of force, or the management of shared natural resources."[85] Just a year after this declaration, many of the same judges did decide a case dealing with genocide and the application of the Convention on the Prevention and Punishment of the Crime of Genocide (*Bosnia and Herzegovina* v. *Serbia and Montenegro*).[86]

If we are going to ask more of the ICJ and other international courts, then we need to better appreciate what international courts are and whom they serve. Our expectations of those who serve as judges in these forums should be realistic. To achieve that, we need to destigmatize unrealistic assumptions about how judges can and should engage in judicial decision making. Although this task may prove hard to carry out, it is high time we recognize that judges, like all of us, are human.

5

Human Choice at the UN Security Council

That's me. I am the United States when I speak.

Former US Ambassador to the United Nations John Danforth[1]

5.1 UN Security Council approves no-fly zone for Libya. Credit: Monika Graff/ Stringer/Getty Images

On October 10, 2019, the UN Security Council met in an emergency closed-door session at UN headquarters in New York City.[2] One day prior to that, Turkish president Recep Tayyip Erdoğan had ordered a ground invasion into northeastern Syria, claiming that Kurdish fighters, instrumental US allies in the fight against the Islamic State, posed a terrorism threat to Turkey.[3] Days earlier, President Donald Trump, acting against the advice of his top military leaders, had ordered US troops out of the region, clearing the way for Turkey's invasion. In spite of the illegal nature of Turkey's actions, the council did not reach an agreement to condemn Turkey's use of force in Syria and its Kurdish-controlled northern border region. Russia and the United States allegedly had blocked the resolution.[4]

From an international legal perspective, such a choice by two permanent Security Council members is concerning. Turkey appeared to have violated the rules of international law. Per the UN Charter, which established the Security Council and its unique powers, nations are prohibited from using force against other nations.[5] There are two exceptions. First, use of force is legally permissible when authorized by the Security Council, pursuant to Article 42 of the UN Charter.[6] This did not happen in the case of Turkey. Second, use of force is permitted when it is necessary for a nation's self-defense.[7] Turkey's allegations that Kurdish-controlled regions on its border and in Syria posed a terrorism threat were an attempt to satisfy this second condition. But those grounds were weak.

The council's inability to condemn Erdoğan's use of force in Syria reveals, not surprisingly, that the Security Council does not make resolutions and other choices based on international law alone. The fifteen nations that serve as members of the Security Council form their choices based on political and national interests in ways that can elude and sometimes contravene international law.

This raises an old thorn for international law, namely, its struggle to rule over and enforce state behavior.[8] International legal scholars have studied this struggle in various ways, such as examining how the Security Council's informal practices have been employed to support state behavior that lacks justification under international law.[9] Scholars have also studied the Security Council by analyzing state behavior over time.[10] As discussed in Chapter 2, international legal scholarship focuses on state behavior and the state as the unit of analysis. It does not, at present, focus on how aspects of human choice, such as emotion, bias, and empathy, may shape or explain the decisions the Security Council takes or decides not to take.

The same critique can be made, more generally, of the rich array of research on the Security Council found in international relations and political-science scholarship. Scholars have analyzed the Security Council through rational choice theory,[11] political dimensions,[12] and practical approaches that consider the council's practice over the years.[13] Scholars have examined the council's behavior by using theories of international organizations, by evaluating the council as a collection of individual countries, and by considering dynamics in the council between the permanent and the nonpermanent members.[14] Social constructivists and other scholars study how various forms of communication, such as political deliberation and legal argument, influence decision making in international organizations.[15] Some frameworks consider people as the units of analysis, analyzing how people empowered to choose understand their choice – whether, for example, as a vote or as a decision justified by norms or values.[16] But, on the whole, international relations, like international law, focuses on the state as the basic unit of analysis.

This chapter takes a different perspective. I aim to apply insights about human choice as a way to further understand Security Council decision making. My central assumption is that understanding the council's decision making requires looking not only at the behavior of states but also at the behavior of the powerful people who represent and run those states. For example, was the US decision at the Security Council to block any resolution condemning Turkey a result of state behavior? Or was it the result of the personal choices of President Trump or his advisors? Who made the decision and who influenced the decision makers? These questions get at my view that state behavior can be better understood when we account for the preferences, power, and choices of individual people who play a central role in representing a state. Of course, it is true that such decision makers act as agents of their state. But it is also true that they do so as human beings prone to aspects of human choice.

Every diplomat is aware of this duality, which was neatly expressed by US Ambassador to the United Nations John Danforth in the epigraph that begins this chapter. Politicians and diplomats have long understood the need to take account of the human actor alongside the state actor when conducting international diplomacy and negotiations.[17] I have experienced this firsthand as a US delegate to the United Nations Compensation Commission (UNCC) and as a low-level member of various US negotiating teams. Early in my government career, my boss at the US Trade Representative's Office formulated US negotiating positions by considering the interagency process, the interests of each constituency and the interests of the nation. However, she also wisely took into account what she could learn about the people on the other side of the negotiating table, particularly what would influence their negotiating tactics and interests.[18] It was there that I first learned that making international decisions in political forums involves more than law or politics. It involves people.

THE UN SECURITY COUNCIL IN CONTEXT

When faced with a threat to global peace brought about by an aggressive leader or countries on the precipice of war, the world needs someone to turn to. Under international law, that someone is the group of fifteen women and men who represent their nations on the UN Security Council. Collectively, these individuals and the countries they represent have the power and responsibility to make choices to maintain international peace and security. But the world didn't always have such a group. Historically speaking, it is a recent development.

The origins of the Security Council date to the start of the twentieth century, when leaders around the world pondered the question of whether or not there should be some sort of world government. Such global governance would require an authority to enforce the rules. However, nations were reluctant to forgo their sovereignty by subjecting themselves to a higher power. When US President Woodrow Wilson sought to establish the League of Nations after the First World War, nations could not agree on the structure or powers of an enforcement arm of the new international organization. Thus, it had none, relying instead on the powerful nations of the day to carry out the enforcement of sanctions. Discomfort and disagreement with this model were important reasons the US did not ratify the Treaty of Versailles at the Paris Peace Conference, thus preventing it from joining the League. Samuel Flagg Bemis opined, "[t]he League of Nations has been a disappointing failure. . . . It has been a failure, not because the United States did not join it; but because the great powers have been unwilling to apply sanctions except where it suited their individual national interests to do so, and because Democracy, on which the original concepts of the League rested for support, has collapsed over half the world."[19] By the start of the Second World War, the League was in peril. It formally ceased to exist on April 18, 1946, when it was dissolved into the United Nations.

The Second World War brought about geopolitical instability and personal tragedy on a global scale. During the war, world leaders began to negotiate what the postwar world order should look like and to develop the idea of a body that could enforce the norms and rules agreed to by nations. At the 1943 Tehran Conference, US President Franklin D. Roosevelt, UK Prime Minister Winston Churchill, and Soviet Premier Joseph Stalin largely mapped out the central tenets of what would become the Security Council. They decided that the council would consist of four permanent member states (France, Union of Soviet Socialists Republics, the United Kingdom, and the United States) that would act as the world's policemen and hold the extraordinary power to veto decisions made by the larger council. After further negotiation, China was added as the fifth permanent member; collectively these nations are known as the permanent five, or P5.[20] In addition, ten nonpermanent member states would serve two-year terms. This arrangement was codified into international law at the signing of the UN Charter in San Francisco in the fall of 1945. The charter gave the Security Council the "primary responsibility for the maintenance of international peace and security."[21] Based at the UN headquarters in New York City, the council makes (and fails to make) decisions, shaping international law and, at times, the fate of humanity.

The council's powers are broad.[22] The United Nations is the international legal system's "law-enforcing collective security organization," and, within it, only the Security Council has the power to authorize the use of force under certain conditions.[23] Furthermore, the council is distinct among political bodies in the United Nations in that it is the only organ whose resolutions are legally binding on all member states.[24] The scope of situations that come before the council and require decisions is defined in Article 39 of the UN Charter. It provides that the council "shall determine the existence of any threat to the peace, breach of the peace, or act of aggression and shall make recommendations, or decide what measures shall be taken in accordance with Articles 41 and 42, to maintain or restore international peace and security."[25] As the negotiating history of the UN Charter reveals, in the 1943 plan the drafters intended the council to have the authority to "determine the existence of a threat or act of aggression, and . . . to institute measures to repress such threat or act."[26] In Security Council Resolution 660, for example, the council declared Iraq's invasion of Kuwait a breach of international law, demanded immediate withdrawal, called for immediate negotiations, and set up the UN Compensation Commission (UNCC) to process claims and to pay for losses resulting from the invasion.[27]

The rationale behind empowering the Council with such widespread and unconstrained authority is an artifact of the political moment in which the United Nations was established. In the aftermath of the Second World War, the victorious nations sought to establish an international legal system capable of preserving peace and security. The UN Charter, which outlaws the aggressive use of force, and the council, which possesses the exclusive right to authorize military action to deter such breaches of the peace, were the primary means to this end. The charter did not, however, define certain key terms such as "peace" or "security," setting the stage for decades of debate about the meanings of these important ideas.[28]

DECISION MAKING AT THE SECURITY COUNCIL

Everything that the Security Council does (or does not do) involves aspects of human choice. The most obvious example is making decisions. The council makes decisions by voting, through consensus, by delegation and through the use of the veto. The UN Charter and the council's provisional rules of procedure set forth the process.[29] When the council is deciding a procedural matter, there must be an affirmative vote by nine of the fifteen members, as required by Article 27 UN Charter.[30] Procedural decisions include adopting an agenda item, voting to hold a meeting in a different location, or approving an annual report. Decisions on "all other matters" require an affirmative vote by nine of the fifteen members and the concurring votes of the five permanent members.[31] Of course, the P5 have veto powers, which they can use to block resolutions or to prevent a matter from coming up for a vote.[32] This becomes a form of decision making in itself. During the council's early years, members disagreed on the difference between procedural and substantive matters, a difference the UN General Assembly aimed to clarify in its 1946 resolution on the matter.[33] That resolution also advises P5 members on the council to constrain their use of the veto and to consult one another on matters before voting.[34]

The veto power was controversial from the start. The United States, France, the United Kingdom, the Soviet Union, and China agreed early on that the veto power would not only safeguard their national interests within the United Nations, but also make the nascent organization viable.[35] The United States insisted on the veto power at the Dumbarton Oaks Conference in 1944 in order to obtain congressional approval (and thus avoid the mistakes made several decades earlier when the US Senate refused to accept US participation in the League of Nations).[36] However, many other nations resisted the veto or sought to limit its effects at the San Francisco conference when the UN Charter was signed.[37] They were largely unsuccessful.

These power differences among nations affect the council's formal decision making. International Crisis Group's UN Director Richard Gowan reflects that "[t]he reality is that the more important the decision in the Security Council, the fewer the states that are involved in it. When you get to a really crucial moment like the Syrian chemical weapons crisis, that's not even the P5 making the decisions, that's the U. S. and Russians. After the 2013 [North Korean] nuclear test the Council actually came up with a pretty tough resolution, but that was negotiated bilaterally by the U.S. and Chinese. Then the other P5 countries got it and then the rest of the council just waved it through."[38] Colin Keating, former New Zealand ambassador to the United Nations, reports that "[t]here are many points of view in the Security Council, and no permanent alliances on anything. There are a series of key positions that need to be accommodated, and this is getting more scary for countries that don't have a clear sense of where they stand internationally or where their next aid check is coming from."[39] These dynamics have intensified in recent years.

In addition to making formal decisions that result in resolutions if they pass, the council engages in informal decision making in a number of ways. The

Security Council may conduct public meetings (for which official records are published) and private meetings (for which the secretary-general keeps one unpublished copy of the official record). Members of the council also engage in informal consultations that are exclusive to council members, informal interactive discussions, and Arria-formula meetings to which non-council members may be invited. In certain cases, the council's decisions take the form of nonbinding written statements issued following informal consultations that have resulted in a consensus. The president of the council typically issues a "statement on behalf of the Council" that makes a recommendation or communicates a view about a specific situation.[40] Although these statements are nonbinding, they can have a legal effect; for example, the council may determine that a state has violated its obligations under international law or change the scope of sanctions.[41]

The council also comes to decisions by delegating its own authority to a subsidiary body, often because it determines that such a body is better suited to make decisions on a particular matter.[42] The UNCC, for example, was developed as a subsidiary organ of the council to adjudicate and process claims brought by victims of Iraq's illegal invasion and occupation of Kuwait. The council has also delegated decisions to its Sanctions Committee, which has a successful record of making decisions quickly. For example, on February 26, 2011, the Security Council established a committee to oversee the council's travel bans and economic sanctions in against Libyan officials.[43] Then, when the new provisional government took power in December 2011, the council rapidly reached a consensus in favor of easing these measures. Outsourcing decision making through delegation provides the council with more procedural flexibility than it would otherwise enjoy, because subsidiary bodies employ their own decision-making practices.[44]

Finally, people beyond the official council members exercise some influence over Security Council activities. First, a permanent staff assists the work of the council, including the Secretariat of the Security Council and the Security Council Affairs Division of the UN's Department of Political and Peacebuilding Affairs. The council also has set up staffed subsidiary bodies, ad hoc bodies, and committees, which address counterterrorism, nonproliferation of nuclear weapons, sanctions, and other concerns. Second, each state party member of the Security Council has its own team, consisting of an ambassador or a high-level representative, legal advisers and additional staff. These teams typically operate out of the permanent mission of their state to the United Nations. Third, being a part of the United Nations, the Security Council has formal and informal communications with the UN General Assembly, the UN secretary-general, and other UN organs. Fourth, countries from around the world may attend UN Security Council open meetings under certain conditions, even though they are not permitted to vote. And fifth, the council has set up a number of mechanisms, such as Arria-formula meetings, informal dialogues, and visiting missions, to gather information from individuals or organizations with relevant knowledge and expertise. Understanding the organizational and procedural structure of the Security Council helps us grasp how many people are involved in its function. A decision by the council is the result of many human choices.

CHOOSING TO INTERVENE IN LIBYA

By far the most contentious decisions the council makes concern whether or not to authorize the use of force according to the authority given to the council under Chapter VII of the UN Charter. It is here that the P5 members' capacity to use the veto becomes most apparent to the public. Russia (and previously the Soviet Union) has used its veto power the most frequently since the founding of the United Nations.[45] The USA comes in second.[46]

In this regard, something extraordinary happened at the Security Council on March 17, 2011. The council passed Resolution 1973, which authorized member states "to take all necessary measures ... to protect civilians" in certain parts of Libya.[47] The resolution passed with ten votes in favor, while five countries (Brazil, China, Germany, Russia, and India) abstained.[48] The language of the resolution was read at the time as an authorization of the use of force under the UN Charter's Article 42 powers. That, in and of itself, was not extraordinary, for the council had authorized use of force many times in the past.[49] The extraordinary thing was the rationale. The resolution allowing member states such authority was based on the purpose of protecting civilians.[50]

Did this resolution represent a historic move by the Security Council, namely, the adoption and exercise of a relatively new idea and principle in international law, the Responsibility to Protect (R2P)? Developed in 2001 by an international commission and adopted at the 2005 World Summit by a majority of nations, R2P reconceptualizes a nation's sovereign rights as having a responsibility to protect its own inhabitants from genocide, crimes against humanity, and other significant harms.[51]

The situation in Libya at the time was volatile and complex. Qaddafi had led the country, intermittently, since his key role in the military coup that removed King Idris and took control of the country in 1969. An early proponent of the pan-African movement, Qaddafi instituted the Islamic calendar, banned the sale of alcohol, and took measures to capture more profits from the foreign oil companies that had long benefited from Libyan oil. A descendant of a Bedouin family, al-Qadhafah, Qaddafi was a complicated political figure. Some saw him as a savior whereas others viewed his anti-colonialist politics as a threat.

By 2011, the Arab Spring movement had reached the streets of Libya. Protests against Qaddafi's brutal rule in the city of Benghazi soon spread throughout the country amid rising fears of an impending genocide.[52] Then Qaddafi gave a speech that would trigger the end of his rule. He called protestors "cockroaches" (language that was used in the Rwandan genocide) and stated he would cleanse Libya "inch by inch, house by house, home by home, alleyway by alleyway."[53] This language reportedly struck senior officials of the Obama administration, including Secretary of State Hillary Clinton, US Ambassador to the United Nations Samantha Power, and National Security Adviser Susan Rice, and set into motion a chain of events that resulted in the ultimate decision to intervene.[54] The actual intervention was led by NATO forces with a coalition of some nineteen nations and took place between March and October of 2011.[55] Operations officially ceased after Qaddafi was killed that October (details about who killed him and how remain unclear).[56] In the end, intervention saved some, killed others and left Libya, the region, and the Security Council in turmoil.

Elements of human choice, as defined in this book, were very much present in the choices and decisions that set all of this in motion at the Security Council. I had the opportunity to speak with a person who was directly involved in the decisions that resulted in Resolution 1973. This person has requested anonymity, so I shall refer to my source as R. Recalling the final negotiation on Resolution 1973, R describes the dynamic as "very dramatic, emotional, and full of theatrics" as various permanent representatives to the council made statements.[57] R describes how the council reacted to Qaddafi's violent tactics: "Qaddafi was vowing to wipe out a civilian population, so it felt like a historical imperative in the room for the Council to stop the slaughter from happening. There was a very explicit view that this was why the Council needed to take action and to live up to its responsibilities . . . this is what use of force is for."[58] The council already had unanimously adopted sanctions against Libya and referred international criminal charges to the International Criminal Court.[59] Now it was time to decide if the council would do more. France proposed a Chapter VII use of force in the form of a no-fly zone. Russia, represented by the "very experienced, clever and some-times charming" Ambassador Vitaly Churkin, was in favor of something less than Chapter VII authority.[60] In an evening session attended by some ambassadors, US Ambassador Rice ardently supported a robust resolution that would protect civilians and save lives. There was heat around the table and a sense of urgency. Phone calls were made to various countries' leaders in attempts to get explicit approval for the resolution. In the end, the Security Council passed Resolution 1973, authorizing member states "to take all necessary measures . . . to protect civilians and civilian populated areas under threat of attack in the Libyan Arab Jamahiriya, including Benghazi, ten members voting for the resolution and five members abstaining."[61] Libya has never been the same since.

In reflecting on the adoption of the resolution, R remarked that the council members seemed to feel a historic imperative to prevent Qaddafi's all-out slaughter of his people. Various representatives explicitly stated that stopping Qaddafi was the council's responsibility, that "this is what the use of force is for." But later, when the NATO-led bombing started, R reports, "I personally got choked up." The realization that, in trying to save lives, the council's actions meant that other people were killed, hit R at the human level. R reflects: "It stays with me. Of all my experiences, that moment felt the most impactful and the most unsettling. I felt a causal connection between my work and lives saved and lost." When I asked R how the Libya resolution later impacted the council, R remarked that the council members certainly thought about the project of humanitarian intervention differently, noting that "there often are well-intended but not fully thought through actions that people advocate. Are we actually going to war? What's the end game? What is the goal twenty steps down the road? I felt a sense of accomplishment at the time. Now I wonder if it was the right thing."[62]

R's sense of uncertainty is understandable. It is also complicated. Qaddafi was killed, which saved lives. But the intervention caused the deaths of civilians. Reports of ethnic cleansing and other crimes against humanity by the new authorities in the post-intervention chaos unsettled many. The NATO-led forces that intervened in Libya engaged in military activities that arguably went beyond the authorized scope of the Security Council. A new Libyan government needed to be set up. China and Russia, which both abstained from the original intervention resolution but did not veto it, were not pleased with how matters turned out, seeing the intervention as an exercise in regime change. As former UN Deputy Secretary-General Mark Malloch-Brown suggests: "There was a feeling that NATO used the resolution to go much further than the Russians and Chinese anticipated. The resolution to authorize air strikes turned into a much broader regime-change exercise. It fulfilled the worse fear of those who thought that 'you can never give these guys an unlimited mandate for intervention to rescue civilians from imminent threat without them turning it into a broader mandate to serve their own geo-political objectives.' It reopened the scars of the Iraq invasion."[63] The council's choice in 2011 has had lasting impact, some of it good, much of it bad.

Understanding the context surrounding this decision is critical. Any time the council authorizes the use of force, it is cause for notice and concern. Such resolutions show the Security Council's power at its fullest, a power that was deeply debated when the United Nations was founded. This power rests on legal authority, but it is actualized by and through human choice. In this case, a motivating factor for many Security Council members was a conviction that the council should act to save civilians from being murdered en masse by their government. It is also the case that the people and leader in question were from Libya, not a powerful or wealthy nation. Whether one understands this stance as recognition of the need for humanitarian intervention, as an adoption of the principle of the Responsibility to Protect, or both, it is striking because it represented a novel basis for Security Council Chapter VII action. For this reason, the story of Libya points to the need to understand better the many complexities involved in Security Council decision making, particularly when the council authorizes the use of force.

UNDERSTANDING HUMAN CHOICE IN SECURITY COUNCIL CHOICE

The choices and decisions people make are the product of our cognitive processes. As the history of Resolution 1973 illustrates, people make the choices that become the decision of a state, or of the Security Council. Consequently, we must aim to understand human behavior in addition to state behavior if we are to understand fully what goes on at the Security Council or in other bodies that shape international law and the international order. Using this approach, I necessarily do not assert claims of actual representation or causality. I cannot claim that the French ambassador decided this way or that because of a certain emotion, for example. Instead, the following section illustrates how insights about human choice can illuminate understandings about Security Council decision making, deepening our knowledge along the way.

A human-choice approach complements existing work in political science and international relations that has focused on understanding how leaders make decisions and their individual influence on foreign policy and statecraft.[64] Relevant scholarship covers situational factors, organizational structure, and leadership position as well as the behavior and decision making of leaders as individuals through psychology.[65] For example, the well-known book *Groupthink* employs psychology to explain how the process of foreign-policy decision making can be deeply flawed, leading to equally flawed outcomes.[66] This psychological approach has given us such theories as the Hobbesian Trap, which provides a theoretical explanation for why President John F. Kennedy and Soviet Chairman Nikita Khrushchev both chose to escalate toward preemptive nuclear strikes to eliminate the threat they thought the other posed during the Cuban Missile Crisis.[67] The theory is that fear, not rational thought, drove the impulse to strike preemptively.

Overall, much of this literature takes a US-centric perspective, and, as such, may have limited application to the understanding of human behavior within the globally diverse Security Council. The Security Council makes decisions that are political and also one's that are quasi-judicial. This puts analyzing the Security Council in a class of its own as a decision-making forum.

TRUST AND INTERPERSONAL RELATIONSHIPS

The study of personal factors, cognition, and behavior is vital to understanding human choice in the real world. Who you are matters, in diplomacy and in life. For example, former Secretary of State and Ambassador to the United Nations Madeline Albright has described how being a woman, often the only woman in the room, influenced how she did her job as the representative and voice of the United States.[68] An old friend of mine, former Thai ambassador to the United Nations Kantathi Suphamongkhon, always says that effective diplomacy requires a "personal touch" in order to establish good relationships with people.[69] Good relationships, in turn, can lead to agreement. Having served as a US delegate to the United Nations myself, I have seen firsthand the importance of relationship building in making agreements and deals. Of course, this is true in boardrooms, classrooms, and places beyond the United Nations. We all have had experiences when we reached a deal or agreement with someone because we liked them, they liked us, or both.

One factor associated with good relationships is trust, or the "assured reliance on the character, ability, strength or truth of someone."[70] Neuroeconomic research has shown that trust is linked to economic prosperity of nations and to successful outcomes for people who work together.[71] The basic idea is that trust "profoundly improves organizational performance by providing the foundation for effective teamwork and intrinsic motivation."[72] The Security Council is not a company, but it is an organization whose members have to work together to reach decisions. Trust in this setting affords good professional relationships, which help a group achieve its goals. Trust can also facilitate an increased exchange of information and, at the council, information is power.

Trust at the council is tricky. Many council dynamics come into play. First, the five permanent members have decades of institutional relationships on the council, whether good or bad. Certain practices, such as circulating a draft position to P5 allies before presenting them to the larger council, come into play. Second, P5 nations with long-serving diplomats on the council have an advantage over P5 nations whose diplomats are relative newcomers, in that the old hands know how to get things done based on experience and memory. For example, R reports that Russian Ambassador Churkin was on the council for "a very long time and would abuse that to new people. That is how it worked. It was rough but useful."[73] Third, nonpermanent council members are disadvantaged on both of these two fronts, as they only serve for a short time. This, in turn, reinforces the power differences between the two groups, and that influences decision making.

A human-choice approach values understanding factors like trust that can influence the choices people make at the cognitive level. For example, Harvard psychologist Howard Gardner describes how people change their minds when presented with new information or because they like someone.[74] Mapping such research onto decision moments at the Security Council presents problems but, anecdotally, stories about how the identity of an individual matters to others in the room abound. According to R, a type of individual influence took place at the Security Council in November 2013. The African Union had sent a letter asking the council to defer the cases before the International Criminal Court looking into the election in Kenya, pursuant to Article 6. Only seven council members were in favor of granting the request, fewer than the nine votes necessary, but several states pushed for a vote anyway. Then, in a "dramatic moment" by council standards, the representative from Rwanda accused the council of not caring about Africa and abandoning it.[75] He received a standing ovation from several other members, resulting in a split in the council between African nations and their allies, and other representatives. Because of the Rwandan genocide, the Rwandan representative had the legitimacy and moral authority to speak on the matter.

Little research and even less agreement exist concerning the accuracy of relating research on individual cognition and behavior to outcomes of an international organization such as the Security Council. The logic is that a nation takes its position and the diplomat merely represents that position at the council. As we know, a representative at the Security Council is not the sole decider of the position of their nation. The ultimate decision maker, often the leader of that nation, is not even in the room during discussions. However, the representative does have the power to persuade others and to influence which positions are taken and, consequently, to affect what choices are made.

EMOTION AND CRISIS

Decisions made during a crisis can differ from those made during ordinary times. Part of the reason for this has to do with the effect that conditions during a crisis can have on human cognition. Political scientists, international relations scholars, and psychologists have long considered multiple theories to explain how emotion can impact thinking during times of crisis.[76] Neuroscience and cognitive studies offer insights as well. We know that decision making involves a variety of cognitive functions in our brains, functions that occur through multiple neural systems operating concurrently or in sequence.[77] We also know that this nonlinear system allows parallel processing of various cognitive activities in the brain, so a person can engage in perceiving and choosing at the same time.[78] For example, if you reach for a hamburger but a yellowjacket lands on top of it, your brain redirects its thought to account for action (reaching) and perception (seeing a threat) at the same time. Recognition of this simultaneity revises the earlier view that the brain processes information sequentially and demonstrates the complexity of cognitive processes involved in decision making.[79] This research also provides evidence that neural activity in decision making interacts with neural activity associated with empathy and with emotion.[80] The research indicates that factors like a sense of urgency and responsibility to prevent genocide, or empathy with people who would be hurt by armed conflict, have the capacity to change what we think by changing how we think. At the cognitive level, we may employ different regions and circuits in our brains because of how we react to external factors.

Returning to the Security Council, during the Libya crisis some of the decision makers certainly felt a sense of urgency and a sense of responsibility. Some of the leaders from P5 nations have acknowledged that they had previously failed to prevent genocide in Rwanda in the 1990s, and certain leaders felt a sense of shame or regret. For example, US President Bill Clinton, reflecting on the Rwandan genocide, said: "[I]f we'd gone in sooner, I believe we could have saved at least a third of the lives that were lost ... it had an enduring effect on me."[81] In terms of timing, there was a sense of urgency surrounding the council's decision that led to Resolution 1973. There may have been passionate advocacy, late-night meetings or last-minute phone calls. In these conditions, people are often tired and stressed. They have less time than they need to think about all the information. These conditions could certainly have an impact on the cognitive aspects of choice. Such considerations are worthy of serious study.

PURPOSE AND VALUES

Despite having the legal authority to do so, the council has difficulty reaching consensus on political choices regarding intervention.[82] One reason is because the council lacks consensus about the reason for intervening. A UN Security Council diplomat explains the problem. International legal rules do play "somewhat of a role ... but [they are] not a predominant force" in shaping political decisions about intervention. "We have something we want to do, the lawyers craft language. [They] don't ever say 'you cannot do the objective you want to do' because it goes against international law. The aim [of intervention] – what we are trying to do – increasingly shapes UNSC decision making about intervention."[83] As an example, the diplomat describes the council's decision in 2013 to authorize MONUSCO (the United Nations Organization Stabilization Mission in the Democratic Republic of the Congo) to use force in the DRC to protect civilians, humanitarian personnel, and human rights defenders.[84] The diplomat explains that the council was not just motivated by each member's national interests. "Few members have national interests in this region. The support for this U.N. mandate was based on other reasons, reasons having to do with concern for human lives. The problem is that international law is invoked to support different and competing decisions. Libya has become synonymous with R2P. People use R2P as a way to create a hierarchy of international legal norms."[85]

R2P, as previously mentioned, is the principle (and emerging norm) in international law that states are not entitled to absolute sovereignty, and therefore the corresponding right to nonintervention, when they directly harm their own civilian population or fail to protect that population from third-party harm. Discussing R2P in 2000, then UN Secretary-General Kofi Annan posed the question: "[I]f humanitarian intervention is, indeed, an unacceptable assault on sovereignty, how should we respond to a Rwanda, to a Srebrenica – to gross and systematic violations of human rights that offend every precept of our common humanity?"[86]

The challenge for the Security Council is that authorizing Chapter VII intervention for humanitarian protection was not envisioned as its original role.[87] However, after the various decisions not to intervene in the 1990s in Rwanda, Kosovo, and the former Yugoslavia, many at the council were filled with a sense of regret. As the Canadian foreign minister at the time, Lloyd Axworthy, put it, "[p]romoting the protection of civilians in armed conflict is no sideshow to the Council's mandate for ensuring international peace and security; it's central to it."[88] During Madeline Albright's era, the Security Council "demanded full respect for international humanitarian law in the protected areas of Bosnia."[89] By the time the council considered the situation in Libya in 2011, members felt a historical imperative to do something, as R recalls, in order to "save lives."[90] This sense of purpose may have helped form the consensus needed for Resolution 1973 to pass. It certainly was the reported motivation behind the council's resolution to use force in the crisis in the DRC. The ongoing war there had killed millions. Many more had been raped, injured, psychologically traumatized, and physically displaced. Their government had failed them. When, in 2013, the UNSC authorized MONUSCO to preemptively use force against rebel groups in order to protect civilians in the DRC, there was a sense that the international community had come through for these people. At the council, people felt "that those killed, various rebels, good riddance."[91] The intervention has been hailed as a success, and this outcome was the one many had hoped for with Libya, but which never came.

CONCLUSION

The UN Security Council is one of the most powerful organizations in the world. It, and it alone, has the authority to decide to use force in nations and on people. For some, the council is viewed as a savior, promising to protect and lay the groundwork for a more peaceful future. For others, blame for the loss of lives lays at the council's feet. As the story of the Security Council's decision to authorize intervention into Libya illustrates, decision making at the council can be a matter of life and death. Recall the account of R, who "got choked up" when bombing began in Libya as a result of Resolution 1973 and who was affected on a "human level" because people died as a result of NATO action.[92] Choices about decisions to intervene with military force in a sovereign nation are difficult to make precisely because they involve human elements in addition to political and legal ones. Understanding why is an endeavor worthy of serious inquiry.

6

Human Choice in Human Rights

[P]eople who have lived through a terrible conflict may be hungry and desperate, but they're not stupid. They often have very good ideas about how peace can evolve, and they need to be asked.[1]

2011 Nobel Peace Laureate, Leymah Gbowee

6.1 Demonstrators for LGBTQ rights in India. Credit: Dibyangshu Sarkar/Contributor/Getty Images

The idea of human rights holds a special place in international law. It stands for a larger, loftier ideal that all people, by virtue of simply being, have certain inherent rights. These rights are meant to form a check on powers that would abuse our inherent freedoms, equality, and dignity. This vision of what human rights can do persists in the places and spaces of international law, however imperfectly, yet far too many human rights abuses continue to take place around the world every day.

Take the stories of Kabba and James. Kabba Williams was only seven years old when he was taken into the Revolutionary United Front and forced to fight for three plus years. He was later rescued by UNICEF and went on to become a human rights advocate for child soldiers, moving his life journey, in his words, from "a culture of violence to a the culture of peace."[2] James was thirteen when he was conscripted as a child soldier in South Sudan at the hand of his brother in the summer of 1987. Spending seven years in the army, James recalls missing out on his childhood that "it became very dangerous, it became very, very hard." One day, James was shot in the shoulder and remained in the bush that night and later found his way to a refugee camp where there was a school. Today he serves as a child protection officer for the United Nations in Sudan, using his own experience to ensure that other children do not have to experience what he did.[3] James' and Kabba's experiences reflect the tragic reality that too many children are abducted, abused, and hurt during armed conflict.[4] Their stories also reveal how human behavior is full of the possibility that human rights hopes to impart. Sometimes, those who have been victims turned perpetrators return to serve the cause of human rights, ensuring that what happened to them does not happen to others.

Stories like these are a touchstone for the broader world of human rights.[5] It is full of peril, promise, and potential. It is messy. It is hopeful. It is as complex as we are. Human rights movements and the new norms and laws that they have birthed have given more people greater protections and freedoms. However, progress has been uneven; the landscape of rights and their enforcement is full of peaks and valleys. The protections that extend from international human rights law are neither universal nor uniform. International human rights law still has gaps, leaving certain groups, such as indigenous peoples and minorities, with inadequate protection. Enforcement relies heavily on state consent and good-faith participation, requiring strong political commitment by powerful states that has, in recent years, been lacking.[6]

In this chapter, I explore how the promise of human rights is intrinsically connected to people's choices. In other words, human rights law is inherently human. People choose when they commit acts that violate human rights. People choose when they advocate on behalf of human rights victims. People choose when they adjudicate human rights claims before courts and other legal bodies. People choose when they formulate state consent to a treaty. The groundbreaking decisions that have shaped international human rights law were necessarily the product of the choices that people, acting as decision makers, made. Taking a human choice approach to understanding human rights helps to reveal the connection that exists between people when, for example, a person who has suffered an abuse shares testimony before a court or where diplomats are impressed by the suffering they witness. Perhaps as a reflection of this emphasis on the human, international human rights law, unlike other areas of international law, is often viewed as a place in which passions, emotion, and expressions of humanitarian concern are not merely tolerated but are expected and, at times, encouraged. Herein, we will examine how elements of human choice – such as emotion, empathy, and bias – show up in human rights spaces and scholarship.

A BRIEF HISTORY OF HUMAN RIGHTS

The history of human rights stretches back millennia. In ancient Egypt, some treaties included provisions restricting the use of force.[7] Evidence exists that certain laws in ancient Rome rested on an ethical, benevolent consideration for the well-being of others, or *humanitas*.[8] International law traditionally traces the history of human rights to seventeenth-century Europe, after the publication of Hugo Grotius' 1625 treatise *On the Laws of War and Peace*, the resulting "Grotian Moment," and the Peace of Westphalia in 1648, when leaders of European nations agreed to concepts such as sovereignty, aimed at achieving peace.[9] A little more than a century later, the American Declaration of Independence of 1776 and the French Declaration of the Rights of Man and the Citizen of 1789 sought to secure basic rights and protections for certain men.[10] The Haitian Revolution of 1791–1804, which ended slavery and French colonial rule in Haiti, also marked the power of the quest for freedom and self-determination.[11] Other efforts to affirm the right to life, liberty, and equality followed, through the abolition of the transatlantic slave trade and, later, of slavery, which became one of the first *jus cogens* norms under international law, paving the way for the idea of preemptory norms.[12]

In the modern era, the United Nations Charter of 1945 and the Universal Declaration of Human Rights of 1949 form the foundation of our current international legal framework on human rights. The declaration established core values that have been reinforced through binding treaties covering civil, cultural, economic, political, and social rights.[13] The reason for a universal expression of human rights was expressed by the third secretary-general of the United Nations, U Thant, who said "[e]very human being of whatever origin, of whatever station, deserves respect. We must respect others even as we respect ourselves."[14] Legal protections, norm development, and other gains in human rights have been made by people, from those who negotiated and drafted treaty language to those who protested and suffered.

At the same time, not all people have been allowed to shape what international human rights law is. Many voices and viewpoints were missing from these discourses – and remain so to this day. African-Americans, a historically marginalized minority in the United States, long sought to establish protections against racism through the international human rights framework without success. W.E.B. Du Bois, for example, led a delegation from the National Association for the Advancement of Colored People to the San Francisco conference where the UN Charter was finalized in 1945.[15] Indigenous peoples worked to establish human rights for themselves in the 2007 Declaration on the Rights of Indigenous Peoples. Furthermore, it is extremely difficult to protect the human rights of persecuted peoples who are stateless, such as the Rohingya, through a legal system set up by and for states. Hence, we see the recent case before the ICJ brought by the Gambia against Myanmar on behalf of the Rohingya people.[16] These examples demonstrate how the international human rights movement, for all its promises, fails to protect some of the most persecuted and vulnerable people on our planet.[17]

HUMAN RIGHTS AS HUMAN CHOICE

People who bring, defend, and adjudicate human rights claims at the international, regional and national levels do much of the work of human rights law. In addition to dealing with issues of law and fact, human rights cases in these courts often raise questions about fundamental rights and values.[18] Take the work of the European Court of Human Rights, which was established in 1950 by the European Convention on Human Rights. Today, the court is comprised of forty-seven judges and over 600 other professionals who serve in its registry.[19] The court's caseload is high – numbering over 78,000 cases – and consists of legal disputes between states, by individuals against states, and cases arising out of armed conflict.[20] For this reason, legal decisions about human rights can be highly controversial, and in addition to being emotionally charged, they can also be politically volatile.

One example of this is found in the case of Yassin Kadi, a Saudi resident whose assets in Swiss banks were frozen on the basis of a series of UN Security Council resolutions aimed at addressing terrorism, on the grounds of his suspected ties to Al Qaeda.[21] These resolutions were put into effect through the European Union's adoption of new regulations. Kadi brought the case to the European Court of Justice, which allows claims from individuals, on the grounds that seizing his assets in this way violated his fundamental rights.[22]

The court determined that international law may not supersede fundamental rights that form a part of the European Union's constitutional foundations.

In essence, this meant that the UN Security Council's decision to impose sanctions on Kadi in the interest of addressing terrorism could not override his fundamental human rights to due process. The ECJ was the first court to determine that a UNSC resolution was not superior to fundamental human rights. Advocate General of the ECJ, Miguel Poiares Maduro, opined that "the Court held that the Treaty is not merely an agreement between States but an agreement between peoples of Europe."[23] The ECJ's 2008 judgment was widely regarded in international legal circles as controversial because it elevated human rights above state interests. The decision stands as a signal that human rights can supersede state interests and, in doing so, revives an even older controversy about the appropriate place of human rights in international law.

At the time of writing this book, the world is watching another human rights case, one before the International Court of Justice. Aung San Suu Kyi, who won the Nobel Peace Prize in 1991 as a champion of human rights and who is now the state counsellor of Myanmar and the leader of the National League for Democracy political party, appeared before the ICJ in December 2019 to defend her country against allegations of genocide brought by The Gambia.[24] The world watched the oral arguments at the ICJ with great interest, noting the stark contrast between Aung San Suu Kyi, Nobel Peace Prize laureate, and Aung San Suu Kyi, leader of a nation charged with committing acts of genocide. Many wondered how the person who was a global symbol of human rights could become a global symbol of genocide. The ICJ judges may be struck by this contrast as well, although we will likely never know. Details like these matter for fully understanding choice. A person who believes she engages in principled reasoning when making a decision may approach making choices about human rights differently from a person who approaches decision making from an intuitive process.[25]

The UN Security Council, whose mandate under the UN Charter is to maintain international peace and security, has also taken a modest approach to prioritizing human rights over the years. But, at times, the council has recognized the connection between peace and human rights. In its 2000 landmark resolution 1325, the council recognized the essential link between empowering women and promoting peace and security.[26] The council acknowledged that women bear the brunt of war's harms, including untold human rights abuses, and it also acknowledged that women rebuild societies and help establish peace and security. In 2006, the president of the Security Council continued this trend of linking human rights to peace and security, remarking that the "Security Council attaches vital importance to promoting peace and the rule of law, including respect for human rights, as an indisputable element of lasting peace."[27] Yet in 2010, this language was apparently walked back wherein "[t]he Security Council expresses its commitment to ensure that all U.N. efforts to restore peace and security themselves respect and promote the rule of law."[28] Since then, the Security Council has been returning to its long-held position of leaving human rights affairs to other UN organs, even as states including Turkey and Myanmar use allegations of threats to national security as grounds to commit human rights abuses.

This controversy over human rights' place at the UN reached a peak in 2006 when the UN Human Rights Council replaced the UN Human Rights Commission. The commission was founded in 1947 at the start of the United Nations as the primary body for promoting and protecting human rights.[29] Structurally, it was a subsidiary body of the UN's Economic and Social Council and was composed of fifty-three UN member states. In 2002, the United States was voted off the commission and subsequently criticized for human rights abuses in Iraq and, later, Afghanistan. Israel had also come under criticism for its actions in Gaza and against the Palestinian people.[30] Both countries countered that other nations with abysmal human rights records had not received the same level of scrutiny. Concerns about bias and the politicization of the commission eventually led to its demise. In 2006, the UN General Assembly passed a resolution replacing the commission with a new body, the UN Human Rights Council.[31] In June 2018, the United States withdrew from the council due to the council's "chronic bias against Israel," according to then US Ambassador to the UN, Nikki Haley.[32]

EMOTION, EMPATHY, AND STRESS

A human choice analysis of international human rights affords us the opportunity to understand human rights successes and failures in new ways, and, in particular, it provides a reading of human rights law through the choices of people who work on and in human rights. To see these choices, we may look to *travaux préparatoires* to revisit choices made during negotiations of human rights treaties. For example, the negotiation of the International Convention on the Elimination of All Forms of Racial Discrimination (ICERD) treaty reveals the disagreements that representatives had over the meaning of racial discrimination, which helps explain why, in the end, the treaty only names apartheid and racial segregation as specific forms.[33] We may look to people who have survived human rights abuses and listen to their experiences about their loss and need for remedy. We may look to adjudicators who, in deciding a case, also determine how much of the raw reality of lived experiences they experience. In these ways, and others, we begin to understand human rights as the culmination of real people's choices, experiences, and even survival. We begin to appreciate just how human the realm of human rights law is.

Let's start by considering why human rights matters can be so charged, controversial, and full of conflict. One reason is that questions of human rights force people to consider what their own values are and why we have disagreements about them. Take gender discrimination against women. International law has well-established norms against discrimination, including on the basis of gender, as codified in Art. 1(3) and Art. 55 of the UN Charter.[34] In 1979, the treaty calling for states to eliminate discrimination against women, the Convention for the Elimination of All Forms of Discrimination Against Women (CEDAW), was adopted. Yet enforcement has been modest. The landmark case under CEDAW's enforcement mechanisms, *A.T. v. Hungary*, concerned a woman who was egregiously abused by her husband, to the point where she was admitted to the hospital, raising concerns about how extreme human rights abuses have to be to trigger protections under the treaty.[35]

Today, discrimination remains a daily occurrence for billions of women and girls around the world. Why? Well, in spite of signing declarations and ratifying treaties, many states resist implementing international human rights laws that establish equal rights when such laws interfere with domestic matters, cultural practices, and/or religion. Legitimate and illegitimate aspects to these arguments invoke debates about whose views should prevail. Scholars have framed the difference as between universalism, in which rights apply across all nations and peoples irrespective of local context, and cultural relativism, in which local contexts determine how rights apply.[36]

A common example here is the right to education for children. Under universalism, the state is responsible for requiring all children under a certain age to attend school and is also responsible for supplying schools and teachers. Yet, in practice, this has resulted in harm. Consider a nomadic reindeer herding community that moves seasonally with its herd. Under the rationale of enforcing the human right to education, a state may forcibly remove children of this community from their parents to live in a city where there is a school, causing harm to the children's health and well-being. A cultural relativist view would demand alternatives that protect these children. Of course, a relativist view may also be used to remove protections from designated groups. Male Taliban leaders have used a relativist view to claim that women and children will not be afforded certain human rights because doing so violates cultural values.[37]

For another example of the conflicts that arise around human rights, we can look to the negotiation of ICERD, which came together in 1965, two years after the Declaration on the Elimination of Racial Discrimination.

The civil rights movement in the USA was at its height; the horrors of apartheid in South Africa were ongoing; and widespread independence movements were rejecting colonialism. During negotiations, state representatives disagreed on the type and extent of racial discrimination that should be enumerated in the treaty.[38] They also disagreed on how to characterize ethnic and religious discrimination, as well as discrimination that combined the two, such as anti-Semitism and Islamophobia, leading representatives to argue that if the treaty would not enumerate all forms of racial discrimination then it should not enumerate any. The final text of ICERD generally prohibits racial discrimination and only mentions apartheid and racial segregation by name.[39] These examples illustrate how individuals and their particular values and beliefs shaped the form and meaning of two essential human rights treaties.

Given these levels of disagreement, it is not uncommon to see anger, sorrow, pain, empathy, and other emotions in human rights spaces. Victims of horrendous injustices shout out their anger and cry out their pain to human rights bodies, commissions, and courts.[40] Diplomats make passionate pleas to different UN bodies, imploring action in the face of massive humanitarian crises.[41] Heads of state invoke human rights norms when making appeals to the international community. We can find an example in the Inter-American Court of Human Right's[42] 2012 landmark decision in *Atala Riffo and Daughters* v. *Chile*.[43] Atala Riffo was a Chilean citizen and federal judge who had divorced her husband and gained custody of their three children in 2001. When she came out as a lesbian a year later, her husband sought to regain custody of their children. The Supreme Court of Chile granted him custody on the grounds that Atala Riffo's decision to date women would pose a risk to her children. The Inter-American Court determined that this decision violated rights afforded to individuals on the basis of equal protection under the law and found that, on these grounds, Chile (and other state parties to the Organization of American States) was obliged to legalize same-sex marriage under national law.[44] In doing so, the Inter-American Court was the first court to articulate a state obligation to legalize same-sex marriage under international human rights law.[45] Jorge Contesse, who served as co-counsel for Riffo during her hearing at the Inter-American Commission of Human Rights, recalled that "like many hearings that come before the IACHR, [this one was] charged with emotion."[46]

I was fortunate to witness a similar dynamic at the November 2018 Inter-American Human Rights Commission hearings at the University of Colorado School of Law. The families and advocates of people who have been disappeared along the US border and of indigenous women in Alaska who had been killed made emotion-laden pleas to the commissioners.[47] People cried and called out in anger. Attendees held signs in protest. This environment is not at all uncommon at commission hearings and most people in the room seemed to expect it. What was perhaps less expected, but deeply appreciated by attendees and families of the missing, was the response of the commissioners. Margarette May Macaulay and Flávia Piovesan acknowledged people and their losses and thanked them for sharing their emotions alongside their legal claims. This was a marked difference from my experience before arbitrators and judges in other international tribunals, and I believe that both the nature of human rights violations and the ability of individual claimants to appear and to be heard considerably changes the dynamics.

To better understand dynamics such as the ones that I witnessed, we can engage the research on emotion and empathy that investigates why and how people influence each other. Recall Chapter 3's introduction of empathy as a system of flexible conceptual representations that translate thought into emotion.[48] Here, we find evidence that we can, quite literally, feel one another's pain. A 2017 study, for example, investigated the ways that our brains do this and observed that someone else's pain can invoke our own cognitive pain response, as if we experienced the same pain ourselves.[49]

Whether pain, anger, joy, or frustration, our emotional response to something can be expressed as a feeling, a behavior, or both.[50] The internal factors involved in emotional responses include automatic, hormonal, and behavioral components.[51] If you are walking down the street and a barking dog runs toward you, you may have an automatic response of a rapid heartbeat, which would facilitate a rapid physiological response. Your body may produce epinephrine and norepinephrine, hormones that increase blood flow to your muscles. Behaviorally, these components prepare your body to run or to fight. At the neurological level, each of these components involves distinct brain regions and neural systems. The integration between automatic, hormonal, and behavioral components, however, is believed to take place in the amygdala. Our ability to regulate our emotions is linked to neural activity in the prefrontal cortex, which is also involved with higher-level cognitive functions involved in choice. Thus, at a very general level, cognitive activity associated with emotion and choice can be linked in our brains, in the amygdala and in the prefrontal cortex.[52]

Certain emotions can cause us to feel stress, which also affects our choices.[53] Prolonged stress causes damage to our bodies and to our brains. For example, the overproduction of glucocorticoids, a class of steroids, in our bodies is harmful and can cause decreased immune function or high blood pressure. Stress can also harm our brains, producing cognitive deficits, symptoms of which include anxiety, insomnia, depression, hallucinations, and delusions.[54] Stress also increases the release of the neurotransmitter norepinephrine in areas of the brain that involve cognitive activity related to choice, such as the prefrontal cortex, which is why stress can impact a person's decision making in a variety of complex ways.[55] Because of the ways that we experience emotion, empathy, and stress, human rights spaces provide a rich environment in which to study how people's choices, not just state actions, inform and influence the law.

CONCLUSION

People shape what human rights law is and how it operates in our world. For example, when CEDAW was being negotiated, discussion about the terms of that treaty revealed that even the delegates responsible for negotiating it had discriminatory views.[56] In attempting to justify the differential treatment in national law for women and men, a male representative from the Philippines remarked that the severe penalties for the crime of rape were imposed in his country to protect "the honor of a husband, father or brother."[57] His view that it is necessary for law to recognize difference based on gender was not at all uncommon.

We also see direct influence by individual officials who must decide the fate of many in real time. Shashi Tharoor, former UN under-secretary-general for communications and public information, described working in Singapore at the height of the Vietnamese refugee crisis, when people came by boat to Singapore and were taken to UN refugee camps there:[58] "[W]e were dealing with actual human beings, and I could put my head on the pillow at night knowing that what I did made a real difference in people's lives – people I could see and feel and meet and touch and actually talk to. That kind of direct connection, that's something that UNHRC [UN Human Rights Commission] affords that's truly extraordinary."[59] Tharoor's recollection illuminates how such direct and often intimate contact between decider and decided on influences human rights.

In such human rights stories, we see moments when people bare their human qualities in the choices they make as judges, advocates, diplomats and more. We see connections forged between those who have suffered and those empowered by international law to alleviate said suffering. We see empathy, emotions of all kinds, and stressful moments. We see how personal views and values have the capacity to shape the reach of the law. In these ways, and more, we see how human rights law is shaped by the many brave people who work to make its promise more of a reality.

PART III

The research presented in Part I and the examples presented in Part II demonstrate how complex human choice can be. Our emotions, our values, our biases, our experiences, our memories, and many other factors influence the choices we make and how we make them. Insights from neuroscience, psychology, cognitive studies, and other fields teach us about ourselves and reveal how many mysteries concerning the human brain, behavior, and experience remain. This book has endeavored to link knowledge about human choice to knowledge about international law and how we understand it. Starting from the position that treaties, custom, general principles, and judicial opinions, all sources of international law, are formed by choices people make, this book has argued that understanding human choice is fundamental to understanding international law. We have learned why emotion changes the way our brain accesses memories, makes judgments, or processes predictions. We have learned that, from a cognitive perspective, empathy can influence the neural pathways our brain employs. We know that bias, of many kinds, is real and correlates to brain activity in our amygdala. We also know there are limitations to these findings. Not all brains operate in the same way, and future research will both confirm and overturn existing findings. But it is true that choice involves much more than merely thought or reason.

In Part III, we take up what this human choice analysis means to and requires of international law. Chapter 7 explores implications for professional cultures in international law, and Chapter 8 examines implications for the future of international law and our world. These two chapters begin a conversation about the ways that knowledge about human choice impacts how we think about and carry out the work of international law.

7

Changing the Culture of Choice

Imagine a world where we are linked, not ranked.

Gloria Steinem[1]

7.1 Love in the city. Credit: MirageC/Getty Images

Given what we now know and understand about the complexity of human choice, it is time for international law as a field and as a community of people to embrace the beautiful and messy reality of being human. This chapter calls for a cultural shift in international law and examines some of the advantages and anxieties of such a shift.

Let us return for a moment to the story I shared in the opening chapter, of that candlelit dinner table and the conversation I had with the ICJ judge Z. Recall that we were speaking of a case that the ICJ had taken up concerning an allegation made in 1999 by the Democratic Republic of the Congo that Rwanda had engaged in genocide along the border, highlighted by the fact that Rwanda itself had suffered gravely from genocidal acts less than a decade earlier. Despite the courteous and elegant nature of the dinner, our conversation had turned tense. We both understood the legal basis for the court's determination that it did not have jurisdiction in this case: Rwanda had consented to the ICJ's jurisdiction to adjudicate disputes when it had ratified the Genocide Convention.[2] Our disagreement was less about law, I think, than about values. Of course, I cannot ask Z this question, so I do not know what Z's answer would be. My answer, however, is one that the ICJ's role extends beyond mere international adjudicator toward the realm of guarantor of justice.[3] As the judicial organ of the United Nations, the ICJ has a role to play in upholding the UN-based international order. The separate opinion of judges Higgins, Kooijmans, Elaraby, Owada, and Simma, expressed their own dissatisfaction in the matter, opining "[i]t is a matter for serious concern that at the beginning of the twenty-first century it is still for States to choose whether they consent to the Court adjudicating claims that they have committed genocide."[4] Z's position was that the law did not allow a different outcome and he then responded, "What would you have me do?"

So what were Z and I arguing about? The simple answer is that we disagreed about the choices that the ICJ judges made in this case. A deeper answer is that we disagreed more fundamentally about how ICJ judges should make choices. An even more reflective answer is that we held different views about how people make choices. This book has responded to all three layers of this conversation, starting with the last. If we understand human choice as the sum of complex processes that science tells us it is, then we must revisit assumptions and views about the choices humans make in international law. The difference concerns how an ICJ judge thinks he makes a decision, how those in the field think judges should make their decisions, and how people actually engage in cognitive activity that produces a decision.

My own dinner experience is not unique. I am reminded of an important lecture given by the late, great professor and judge, David Caron, who described the challenge facing international law as a "scene at a dinner party where all appears serene but then a seemingly minor comment gives rise to a harsh response; it is that moment when there is a glimpse of a serious disagreement beneath the surface that has bubbled up unexpectedly."[5] Caron called on international law to better understand and to acknowledge the work that adjudicators do and how they do it.[6] In his view, there was a fundamental and under-recognized tension between the function of international courts and tribunals and the task of judges and arbitrators, whom he referred to collectively as adjudicators. Caron cautioned against expecting judges to develop international law. He described this as a social function and noted how judges are criticized when decisions are (or are perceived to be) made on the basis of policy or in service of public interests rather than on the basis of law. He believed that such decisions go beyond the traditional task of international adjudicators.

Under this view, Z's analysis was both accurate and smart. The choice Z made in the case was framed through the lens of her/his task as provided by the court's mandate and authority and the law and facts before Z.

But, as I have argued here, we ought to understand the choices adjudicators (and others) make as the product of who they are and how their brains work. Our choices are shaped by numerous factors at the cognitive level, some of which we are aware of and some of which remain unknown to us. From a human choice perspective, we might think about the tension in the following way: A person who serves as an adjudicator is aware of the need to justify an opinion on the basis of the applicable law and fact, for that is the task. But that adjudicator has views, values, emotions, and biases about cases, especially tough cases, that they either suppress or consider more explicitly in the text of their opinion. In other words, a human choice analysis asks adjudicators, counsel, parties, and the public to acknowledge the realities of human cognition. Of course, judges face internal struggles about what to do in cases that affect the lives of many or the public good.

So, instead of framing our concern around the idea that a judge, in pursuing social considerations, risks going beyond his task and potentially harming the legitimacy of the tribunal, let us consider a different perspective. Let us presume that some judges believe that their task has a social function. What is wrong with that and what is right about it? Can we bring conversations about it into the open? Are there benefits to making implicit cognitive functions more explicit? Should adjudicators, for example, admit and discuss their emotions as they consider a legal case? What would be lost or gained? If it is not preferable for judges to consider their emotions when adjudicating a case, then let it be for well-explored reasons, not because of a flawed premise that a person can simply put aside emotions and apply law to fact in making a choice. As I have said throughout this book, most people's brains simply do not work that way.

In political forums, such as the UN Security Council, the context is different. The people who make the choices that become a Security Council resolution are doing so as representatives of their countries. One country may have a complex interagency process for reaching a position, which then must be approved by the president or leader before the representative conveys it to the council. Another country may have a more streamlined approach.

Either way, realism forces us to recognize that a representative's choice or final position rests on their state's interests, often framed as rational and almost always dependent on considerations about power.

But those who serve as delegates around the table also bring their full selves to bear. They have concerns about their professional reputations and their future careers. Negotiating in advance of a vote, sharing information during a coffee break, maintaining inscrutable body language, these are all choices in the domain of the people serving as representatives. We have to consider how emotion, empathy (or its absence), and bias influence the choices and behaviors of people who work at and serve on the council. Is anger more acceptable than sorrow? Is showing empathy interpreted as weakness?

I do not have the answers to these questions. But, by raising them, I hope to reveal the promise that considering human choice in international law offers – namely, a reconciliation between the realities of being human and the possibilities of embracing our humanness in the practice and study of international law. To achieve this, we need a cultural shift. The problem in international law is that, for decades now, even centuries, these sorts of question were not generally asked. They are not part of the conversation about legitimacy, authority, or power. Instead, the notion of meritocracy, as subjective as it is, is the determining factor in deciding who rises to the level of international legal decision maker, as a judge or diplomat.

A second problem, which we might think of as a challenge, concerns the professional culture in the field of international law. Whether at the ICJ, at the United Nations, in the halls of foreign ministries, among legal scholars and professors of law at universities, or among top arbitrators and counsel who appear before international tribunals, the culture of international law might be described as "civilized." This term itself is problematic. It reminds one of the history of international law created by and for "civilized" nations at the expense of everyone else: of colonialism, of slavery, of oppression. However, the practices of international law communities, in many respects, are rooted in such a traditional, historic, context. Take, for example, the practice of teatime at the Permanent Court of Arbitration in The Hague, where swans swim in the pond, or the diplomatic talks that occur around a tea in the Serpentine Lounge at the United Nations in Geneva, or the formal panels that predominate at the annual conference of the American Society of International Law. Such practices are linked to a professional culture rooted in a history that can stigmatize emotion, empathy, and compassion as weak, and pretend that bias is nonexistent. They can normalize a professionalism so rigid that it gets in the way of meaningful and authentic professional relations. This old and established culture of international law can inhibit practices and conditions that promote effective decision making. In these spaces, where I myself have been, the professional culture sometimes asks people to place their human realities behind a professional veneer.

VALUING HUMAN CHOICE IN INTERNATIONAL LAW

It is time for a new culture of international law, one that recognizes and acknowledges the full spectrum of human cognition and behavior and accounts for that in its own professional culture. It is time for a culture in which it is okay to feel and to talk about feelings, in which people accept without shame that bias is real and then work to overcome it. We need a culture in which empathy, or its lack, is talked about and recognized as a key factor alongside legal analysis when reaching an outcome based on law. Desirable or not, feelings, bias, and empathy are human traits common to us all. It is time for international law to acknowledge and accept its humanity.

Moving toward this new culture of international law matters. It matters for ensuring that the international law of tomorrow is populated by people who represent cultures, nationalities, races, and genders around the world. It matters for ensuring that those in power in international law come from a diverse array of human identities. It matters for making inclusion a reality in the institutions and spaces of international law. It matters for organizational and human health, for progress, and for success.[7]

The time has come for an authentic and profound culture shift in and through international law. The culture I envision can permeate the layers of hierarchy, the array of institutions, and the scope of work across globe. To draw from the title of Simon Sinek's book, it is a culture in which leaders eat last because they make sacrifices for the good of their teams.[8] It is a culture in which empathy not only matters but also is recognized as a key component of success.[9] It is a culture that celebrates the messy reality of emotion.[10] Knowledge alone is not always enough to create change. It will take people to make these changes in the vast, global spaces of international law. In what follows, I provide two guides to help get us started.

THE BASICS OF HUMAN CHOICE

- Human choice is formed when our brains engage in a variety of cognitive activities in order to reach an outcome.
- We call these outcomes "choices," and they can take various forms, including a decision, judgment, assessment, determination, and opinion.
- Our brains take into account a variety of inputs when we make choices. These might include information, memories about past experiences, emotions, empathy, and biases.
- Inputs can change what we choose by changing the cognitive pathways and circuits we engage in reaching a choice.
- Our cognition includes aspects we are aware of and aspects that are hidden.
- Choices are linked to behaviors.
- Emotions can influence choice in ways that are both helpful and harmful.
- Bias, understood as a preference for or an aversion against someone or something, is real.
- Values matter. People often prefer to make choices that align with their values. Values are shaped by our life experiences, good *and* bad; our memories of those experiences; and the emotions embedded in those memories.
- Human choice is complex. There is no unitary system, part, or pathway in our brains for making choices. There are many.

TEN GUIDING PRINCIPLES FOR A HUMAN-CHOICE APPROACH TO INTERNATIONAL LAW

1. Update assumptions about human choice in international law.
2. Understand that choice is more than thinking or knowing. It also includes feeling, believing, and experiencing.
3. Avoid unrealistic expectations, for example, asking a decision maker to not have emotions or to put them aside.
4. Reevaluate assumptions that emotions are bad for decision making.
5. Acknowledge and understand bias.
6. Embrace empathy.
7. Destigmatize vulnerability.
8. Promote a sense of security and safety.
9. Accept the value of different perspectives and experiences.
10. Encourage authentic human engagement.

CONCLUSION

This chapter has explored the ways that the practice and culture of international law is in tension with the realities of human choice, and the reasons why we need a cultural shift to align the two. Recall the story of Kyoto in Chapter 2 and how, possibly, it was Henry Stimson's love for the city that saved it from the atomic bomb. This is a descriptive point. It reveals that emotion has been and is a part of international legal decision making, whether or not it should be. Choices about international law are inherently complex because people are inherently complex. Information can be imperfect. Conditions are subject to change. People may engage in a similar choice in different ways. However, when we acknowledge that it exists, this complexity enhances how we understand international law.

8

The International Law We Need

By believing passionately in something that still does not exist we create it. The non-existent is whatever we have not sufficiently desired.[1]

Nikos Kazantzakis

8.1 Girl paints the word "Future" on a brick wall. Credit: Artur Debat/Getty Images

Our world is going through a period of unprecedented change. In the first twenty years of the twenty-first century, we have faced the rise of terrorism, a global pandemic that shut down the world in three months, and the realization that impacts from climate change are upon us. These changes have sparked protests, movements, and reform. People are waking up to the reality that the future will be different from the past. Such times call on each of us to choose who we are and who we will become as individuals and as a global community. In a crisis, we can either fall apart or fall together.[2]

Enter international law. The very purpose of international law is to help nations meet such challenges through peaceful cooperation. In this pursuit, international law has worked. For example, thanks to the various peaceful means for the settlement of international disputes and the general prohibition on the use of force, wars between nations have declined since 1945 to nearly zero.[3] International law has also failed at times, actively allowing or turning a blind eye to conditions in which human rights abuses and humanitarian crises fester. As such, international law is a tool that serves the interests of those who wield it. But the threats facing the world in the near future threaten to destroy most of us and crash human civilization as we know it.[4] If we are going to survive as a species and as a planet, only cooperation on a massive scale will get us there. To achieve that, many things need to change, including international law.

I am reminded here of the arresting words of then ICJ vice president Stephen Schwebel in his dissent in the Advisory Opinion on the Legality of the Threat or Use of Nuclear Weapons. He said "[m]ore than any case in the history of the Court, this proceeding presents a titanic tension between State practice and legal principle. It is accordingly the more important not to confuse the international law we have with the international law we need."[5] Given the conditions of our present world and the threats we are facing, it is, indeed, time for the people who shape international law through the choices they make to accept the conditions of our global circumstance. For the world, and humanity with it, to survive into the future, we must develop the international law we need.

INTERNATIONAL LAW AS IT WAS

In 1945, nations agreed to a set of common purposes and principles to promote international cooperation, develop friendly relations, and maintain international peace and security. Enshrined in the preamble to the United Nations Charter, these principles, which all nations agreed to uphold, served "to save succeeding generations from the scourge of war, which twice in our lifetime has brought untold sorrow to mankind."[6] Promoting cooperation on a global scale is as necessary now as it was then to save our world.

In this context, international law, in the modern sense, is a tool that can shape and, sometimes, constrain state behavior through a rich interaction of legal rules, norms, processes, and people.[7] International law does its work in a broad geopolitical context where power, authority, and legitimacy are at play. Historically, international law works differently for powerful states and its application cannot be said to be equitable. As Chapter 5 explored, we see such power dynamics play out quite vividly in the political and sometimes quasi-judicial decisions taken up by the UN Security Council. This is unsurprising because international law was designed by states to serve their interests; in other words, international law is built on the foundation of state sovereignty. The principle of sovereignty holds that a state is entitled by law to supreme authority over its territory. This remains a central tenant of international law that political and judicial choices tend to uphold, so much so that a leader of a nation in which millions are suffering human rights abuses may invoke sovereignty to defend that nation from external political or military interference.[8]

In this, we meet the political and practical compromise inherent in international law. Nations would never have agreed, en masse, to an international system of rules more powerful than they. So international law requires state consent. States explicitly consent to be bound by international legal rules when they ratify a treaty. States implicitly consent when a customary rule emerges due to consistent state practice over time with *opinio juris*. Attempts to thrust international law on states without consent rarely affect powerful nations, which use their power to ensure exceptionalism under international law. Sovereign equality, the idea that all nations are deemed equal under international law, remains an aspiration, not a reality.

There is another important feature of international law, and that is who, or what, has the status of legal personhood. In the eighteenth and nineteenth centuries, international legal personhood applied exclusively to states, meaning states had rights and responsibilities under international law.[9] After the formation of the United Nations in 1945, this loose structure of international law became a more formal system, replete with international courts, tribunals, organizations, and other institutions. In 1949, the International Court of Justice recognized that the United Nations was also an international legal person in its Advisory Opinion on Reparations, paving the way for other international organizations to achieve the same status.[10] Despite this nod to inclusion, however, international law remains a system built to serve states, not people. It remains the case today that individual human beings like you and me are not legal persons under international law. We do not have any standing to bring a case before certain tribunals. For all of its progress – new treaties and rights, norm expansion, institutional proliferation, scholarship, and theory – our international legal system was not designed to be accessible or even visible to most of the almost eight billion people on the planet.

INTERNATIONAL LAW AS IT IS

From the Roman concept of *jus gentium*, international law, in its various forms, has long considered the need to protect the rights and interests of people.[11] To do so today, international law has two key features. First is the principle of *jus cogens*, or compelling law.[12] *Jus cogens* is the principle that certain norms, such as the prohibition of the use of force between states or the prohibition of slavery, may not be set aside or derogated from. The second embedded feature is the principle of *erga omnes*, or obligations owed to the international community as a whole.[13] These two general principles are connected. The ICJ, for example, has determined that the right of self-determination cannot be derogated from by states as a *jus cogens* and creates obligations that states owe to all per *erga omnes*.[14] For all of their promise, these two features of international law remain weak in that they are not generally enforced by states or judicial organs.[15] Legal protections for people under international law are subject to the will and consent of states.

However, the world is changing, and so, too, is the state-centricity of international law. A much-needed humanizing turn in international law is upon us. In the late 1990s, Sir Robert Jennings described a "new kind of international law which directly concerns individuals and entities other than States."[16] He noted that this represented "a radical change from the traditional law which protected individuals only in the capacity of aliens, and only then in terms of the injury done not to the individuals but the State of his nationality."[17] Others began to take note of similar trends, documenting how international law has taken, and can and should take account of the needs of everyday people.[18]

Former International Criminal Tribunal for the former Yugoslavia president and judge Theodor Meron describes this humanizing trend in his 2006 book, *The Humanization of International Law*, in which he documents just how and why international law, driven by the principles of human rights and humanity, is "changing and acquiring a more humane face."[19] Of course, the protection of individuals has early roots in the origins of international humanitarian law and international criminal law, starting with reforms to the practices allowed by states during war, such as the 1863 Lieber Code and the 1899 and 1907 Martens Clause of the Fourth Hague Convention on the Law and Customs of War.[20] But, according to Meron, the rights people have because of international law are increasingly being enforced not only against states but also against individuals, representing a change from the mid-twentieth century.[21] The humanization of international law can also be seen in terminology. For example, the law of war is now more frequently referred to as international humanitarian law.

Human rights, an area of international law explicitly committed to the rights of individuals, is also evolving. Human rights emerged as a universal aspect of international law after the Second World War and through the Universal Declaration of Human Rights, and originally envisioned individuals as objects, but not subjects, of international law. Under this model, a state agrees to be bound by a legal rule that creates rights for individuals and obligations for the state.[22] For example, Article 20 of the Declaration asserts a right to freedom of peaceful assembly. Nations that agreed to be bound by this, perhaps through ratification of a subsequent treaty, must not arbitrarily arrest people who gather for peaceful protest.[23]

But the domain of human rights in international law has expanded beyond this state-centric model. As Dinah Shelton explains, the status quo of human rights law has shifted: "[I]n the second half of the twentieth century, a short period of rapid change punctuated the equilibrium and ushered in entirely new doctrines, laws and governing institutions, fundamentally changing the international legal system."[24] Ruti Tietel has described one change as a normative shift that envisions people's needs at the core of legal frameworks. For example, international security is reconceived around human security.[25] Like Tietel, many scholars are shining a light on the need to humanize the work of human rights and acknowledge the value of those who have had their rights violated.[26] Human rights is leading the move in international law beyond the state into the hands of the people.

To end this discussion on how we can conceptualize the current state of international law, let us revisit one of the most dramatic signals of the humanizing turn: the emergence of the Responsibility to Protect Doctrine (R2P) in 2001 and its adoption by nations at the 2005 World Summit.[27] R2P took on some of the problems with a system loyal to state sovereignty. What ought to be done when a leader invoked the principle of state sovereignty and the corresponding principle of nonintervention to avoid accountability for acts amounting to international crimes? The doctrine reconceptualized state sovereignty around a responsibility that governments and their leaders owe to the people. Where a government failed to uphold such a responsibility, its sovereignty was limited, thus allowing the international community to intervene to protect people. In some ways, R2P sought to answer the question posed by the International Law Commission that same year, "whether measures of forcible humanitarian intervention, not sanctioned pursuant to Chapters VII or VIII of the Charter of the United Nations, may be lawful under modern international law."[28]

R2P was as bold as it seems. It aimed to create new legal authority for nations to intervene in other nations.[29] To put this into further context, from the 1990s on, the international community struggled with an adequate response to genocide in Rwanda; ethnic war in Yugoslavia, Bosnia, and Herzegovina; and civil war in Liberia and Sierra Leone (and later in Ivory Coast). The tools provided in the UN Charter of 1945 for war between nations did not fit well for the new kinds of armed conflict the world faced. Traditionally, the UNSC has interpreted its Article 39 authority to include authorization to restore peace (Somalia), to protect a nation against an illegal invasion into its sovereign territory (Iraq's invasion of Kuwait), and to respond to systematic maltreatment of minorities (South Africa).[30] In the face of the changing nature of war, the Security Council's responses became more inconsistent and flawed. Its authorization of the use of force in Libya, described in Chapter 5, revealed R2P in action and the subsequent breakdown of trust, leading to inaction on Syria and in other crises.[31]

What grand lessons might we draw from this? You might argue that state sovereignty wins and efforts to humanize international law too quickly and too broadly fail. Or you might see it another way – that R2P, however imperfect, represents a moment when international law, and those working within it, tried to be more and to do more. Yes, such tries are imperfect and flawed but they keep the spirit of international law's commitment to humanity alive. In dark times, people provide other people with a beacon of hope that conditions can improve. As Hersch Lauterpacht remarked in 1946, "the principle of humanitarian intervention, [is] the principle that the exclusiveness of domestic jurisdiction stops where outrage upon humanity begins."[32] He knew then, as we do now, that an international legal system that allows humanity to suffer in grand and grave ways becomes a tool of destruction, not of peace.

INTERNATIONAL LAW AS IT NEEDS TO BE

When we consider the evolution of international law over time, we see something both obvious and compelling. Great changes to international law are connected to great changes for humanity. New norms emerge after tragedy. New rules emerge after war. New leaders arise from the ashes of hard times before. Antonio Cassese referred to these individuals as "soul leaders" who "could inject new ideas into the fabric of the world community and push through solutions to some of the festering problems currently polluting that community."[33]

What international law needs now are many of these "soul leaders." People who are committed to serve as a force for good and justice in our world. People make and shape international law, so if it is to evolve to meet the challenges of the future, so, too, must we. To start this evolution, we can begin by becoming more aware of ourselves, our limitations, and our possibilities. Whether we are judges, diplomats, state leaders, or advocates, we are all subject to the perils and promise of human behavior. Understanding how thoughts, feelings, and values influence the work we do is an essential part of this mission. International law that is ready to meet current and future threats requires people within it who are also ready. To be ready, judges, attorneys, diplomats, and scholars must be committed not only to upholding international law but also to upholding the foundational principles and purposes that international law exists to serve.

We can begin this journey by asking and engaging the following questions. First, do we value what international law does? Here, we look to international law's first principles, which include dignity, equality, self-determination, justice, peace, and security.[34] Very few would disagree with the normative importance of these values. What we need is a deeper commitment to seeing them through in difficult circumstances. We need a commitment to courage in the face of unchecked power; a commitment to creativity in understanding how law should meet and serve justice; a commitment to people, to those who need protection, to those who have suffered, and those who have died.

Stories remind us why international law exists and the good it can do. They remind us of Raphael Lemkin's narrow escape from Europe to the USA, and his trek in a tattered suit to the Nuremburg Trials to make the case for calling what the Nazis did genocide.[35] They remind us of unnamed Witness J's brave testimony before male judges during the *Akayesu* trial about the rape of her daughter during the Rwandan genocide, leading the International Criminal Tribunal for Rwanda to recognize sexual violence as a part of the indictment.[36] They remind us of countless others, without whose choices and actions the world would be a different, darker place. For all these people, and more, international law must seek to serve humanity better.

Here, we reach a second step in our evolution. It is time to let go of inaccurate and outdated ideas about legal decision making, human thought, and rationality. Irrefutable evidence from a variety of fields shows that the human brain develops emotion, thought, judgment, assessment, and choice in wonderfully complex ways that defy being described merely as rational or irrational. We must also give up ideas that emotions and empathy are somehow bad for decision making. As Chapter 3 revealed, emotion can help and hinder brain activity associated with choice. Context and details are everything.

As our third step, we, the people of international law, must embrace our own humanness. We are human. We are supposed to have emotions. Stress impacts us. Bias is real. We have preferences toward and against others reinforced by our memories and life experiences. We cannot simply separate these factors in our minds and make choices based only on law and fact. We need to change the professional cultures and spaces where such impossible expectations frustrate reality. Recall Chapter 7's discussion of David Caron's concern that, perhaps, too much is being asked of international adjudicators who are constrained in their task by the legitimate function of a court or tribunal. What if we think about this differently? Perhaps too little is being asked of tribunals and other institutions and, most fundamentally, of states that have limited the scope of what such institutions can do from the very start.

CONCLUSION

Human Choice in International Law has sought to identify what it means for human actors to be the creators of international law. It has explored how human beings think, feel, believe, and, ultimately, choose. Furthermore, it has explored what this understanding of human choice might mean for understandings about international law. People create international law. People act on and in international law. Even when a nation decides to consent to a legal rule or norm, it is a person or a group of people who are the central actor within the state actor. To put it more boldly, all international law is essentially human. Unless or until artificial intelligence takes over, human choice remains at the very core of the creation process of international law and the law itself. International law must make the turn, fully and unapologetically, to placing people at the core of what it is and whom it serves. Understanding international law in this new way allows us to recognize and acknowledge the beauty and faults of being human. We are, at times, both the problem and the solution and, in the end, our common survival comes down to human choice.

List of Interviews

1. Georges Abi-Saab
2. Thomas Buergenthal
3. Joan Donoghue
4. Bruno Simma
5. Lucy Reed
6. Laurence Boisson de Chazournes
7. Catherine Powell
8. Interview with R
9. Interview with UNSC Diplomat

Notes

1 INTRODUCTION

1. Hans Kelsen, *Peace Through Law* (New York: University of North Carolina Press by Van Rees Press, 1944), pp. viii–ix.
2. Armed Activities on the Territory Congo (New Application: 2002) (*Dem. Rep. Congo* v. *Rwanda*), Summary of Judgment, 2006 ICJ (Feb. 3).
3. See Case Concerning Armed Activities on the Territory of the Congo (*Dem. Rep. Congo* v. *Rwanda*), Judgment, 2005 ICJ (Dec. 19). Wherein the DRC alleged that Rwandan forces had committed acts of genocide, the court, after considering jurisdictional clauses in the Genocide Convention and the Convention on Discrimination against Women, determined that it lacked jurisdiction to decide the case on the merits.
4. See interview list in Appendix.
5. "Therefore he who bids the law rule may be deemed to bid God and Reason alone rule, but he who bids man rule adds an element of the beast; for desire is a wild beast, and passion perverts the minds of rulers, even when they are the best of men. The law is reason unaffected by desire." Jonathan Barnes, ed., *The Complete Works of Aristotle: The Revised Oxford Translation* (Princeton, NJ: Princeton University Press, 1984), p. 2042.
6. Barnes, p. 2043.
7. Barnes, *The Complete Works of Aristotle*, p. 2042.
8. Barnes, *The Complete Works of Aristotle*, pp. 2042–3: "Therefore he who bids the law rule may be deemed to bid God and Reason alone rule, but he who bids man rule adds an element of the beast; for desire is a wild beast, and passion perverts the minds of rulers, even when they are the best of men. The law is reason unaffected by desire."
9. Public interest and professional engagement in neuroscience is growing. See, generally, Srinivasan Pillay, *Your Brain and Business: The Neuroscience of Great Leaders* (Upper Saddle River, NJ: FT Press, 2011)

(describing how neuroscience is improving performance in the business environment); Eben Alexander, *Proof of Heaven: A Neurosurgeon's Journey Into the Afterlife* (New York: Simon & Schuster, 2012) (exploring how neuroscience helps us to learn more about the modern brain and how it heals); Norman Doidge, *The Brain That Changes Itself* (New York: Penguin Books, 2007) (discussing how the neuroplastic revolution has implications on different aspects of human life); Michio Kaku, *The Future of the Mind* (Toronto: Penguin Random House, 2014) (describing the movement to understand how the human brain functions); T. Swart, Kitty Chisholm, and Paul Brown, *Neuroscience for Leadership: Harnessing the Brain Gain Advantage* (London: Palgrave Macmillan, 2015) (describing the intersection between the brain and decision making); and Gina Rippon, *Gender and Our Brains: How New Neuroscience Explodes the Myths of the Male and Female Minds* (New York: Pantheon Books, 2019) (revealing how neuroscience challenges ideas that brain functions are shaped by gender).

10. Aristotle used the words passion and desire. The study of emotion in neuroscience is known as affective neuroscience.

11. This insight came from my former colleague, Professor Peter Huang, University of Colorado School of Law.

12. See groundbreaking books by scholars António Damásio, *Descartes' Error: Emotion, Reason and the Human Brain* (New York: Penguin Books, 1994); Daniel Kahneman, *Thinking Fast and Slow* (New York: Farrar, Straus, & Giroux, 2011); Michael S.A. Graziano, *Consciousness and the Social Brain* (Oxford: Oxford University Press, 2013); Oshin Vartanian and Dave R. Mandel, eds., *The Neuroscience of Decision Making* (New York: Psychology Press, 2011). For popular press sources, see Barry Schwartz, *The Paradox of Choice: Why More Is Less* (New York: HarperCollins, 2016); Malcomb Gladwell, *Blink: The Power of Thinking Without Thinking* (New York: Little, Brown, & Company, 2005); Jonah Lehrer, *How We Decide* (New York: Houghton-Mifflin Harcourt Publishing Company, 2009); Dan Ariely, *Predictably Irrational: The Hidden Forces That Shape Our Decisions* (New York: HarperCollins, 2008); Sheena Iyengar, *The Art of Choosing* (New York: Twelve, 2010).

13. My previous research on neuroscience, choice, and law includes: Anna Spain Bradley, "Advancing Neuroscience in International Law; in *International Law as Behavior*, Harlan Grant Cohen & Timothy Meyer, eds. (New York: Cambridge University Press, 2021); Anna Spain Bradley, "The Disruptive Neuroscience of Judicial Choice," 9 *UC Irvine Law Review* 1 (2019); Anna Spain Bradley, "Cognitive Competence in

Executive-Branch Decision-Making," *Connecticut Law Review* 49, no. 3 (2017).

14. Recent works use behavioral science to explore how humans make choices include those by Cass Sunstein: *Nudge: Improving Decisions About Health, Wealth and Happiness* (New York: Penguin, 2008); *Choosing Not to Choose: Understanding the Value of Choice* (Oxford: Oxford University Press, 2015); and *The Ethics of Influence: Government in the Age of Behavioral Science* (New York: Cambridge University Press, 2016).

15. Daniel Terris, Cesare P.R. Romano, and Leigh Swigart, *The International Judge: An Introduction to the Men and Women Who Decide the World's Cases* (Waltham, MA: Brandeis University Press 2007); and Armin von Bogdandy and Ingo Venzke, *In Whose Name?: A Public Law Theory of International Adjudication* (Oxford: Oxford University Press, 2016). It also includes works about the UN Security Council such as David Bosco's *Five to Rule Them All: The UN Security Council and the Making of the Modern World* (Oxford: Oxford University Press, 2009) and, more recently, Devika Hovell's *The Power of Process: The Value of Due Process in Security Council Sanctions Decision-Making* (Oxford: Oxford University Press, 2016) (which examines Security Council decision-making and argues that there has been a shift from state-based choices to individual-based choices in the areas of sanctions).

16. Harlan Grant Cohen and Timothy Meyer, eds., *International Law as Behavior* (New York: Cambridge University Press, 2021). Andrea Bianchi, "Fear and International Law-Making: An Exploratory Inquiry," *Leiden Journal of International Law* 32, no. 3 (2019); Luigi Cominelli, *Cognition of the Law: Toward a Cognitive Sociology of Law and Behavior* (New York: Springer Nature, 2018). Work on behavioral economic research is asking similar questions about how emerging research can and should inform government and state decision-making. Adam Oliver's edited volumes *Behavioral Public Policy* (New York: Cambridge University Press, 2013) and *The Origins of Behavioral Public Policy* (New York: Cambridge University Press, 2017) offer two examples.

17. Jean d' Aspremont, *International Law as a Belief System* (Cambridge: Cambridge University Press, 2018); Anthea Roberts, *Is International Law International?* (Oxford: Oxford University Press, 2017); Jens Ohlin, *The Assault on International Law* (Oxford: Oxford University Press, 2015); Ruti Tietel, *Humanity's Law* (Oxford: Oxford University Press, 2011); Makau Mutua, *Human Rights: A Political and Cultural Critique* (Philadelphia, PA: University of Pennsylvania Press, 2002). This book also engages related work in international relations and foreign policy exploring decision-making approaches and state behavior; see Richard

C. Snyder, H.W. Bruck, and Burton Sapin, *Foreign Policy Decision Making* (New York: Palgrave Macmillan, 2002); Gary Goertz, *International Norms and Decision-Making: A Punctuated Equilibrium Model* (Lanham, MD: Rowman & Littlefield, 2003) (offering a punctuated equilibrium framework for how governments make policy decisions and the related influence of international norms and institutions in this context); and Alex Mintz and Karl DeRouen Jr., *Understanding Foreign Policy Decision Making* (Cambridge: Cambridge University Press, 2010); Brian C. Rathbun, *Reasoning of State: Realists, Romantics and Rationality in International Relations* (Cambridge: Cambridge University Press, 2018) Daniel Bessner and Nicolas Guilhot, eds., *The Decisionist Imagination: Sovereignty, Social Science and Democracy in the 20th Century* (New York: Berghahn Books, 2019).

18. In international law, nations are referred to as states. Abram Chayes, *How Nations Behave* (New York: Columbia University Press, 1979), p. 1. It differs from municipal law in how it can be enforced, for without a world police body, the enforcement of international law requires state cooperation. Hersch Lauterpacht, *The Function of Law* (Oxford: Oxford University Press,1933), p. 346 n4; Hans Kelsen, *Peace Through Law* (Chapel Hill, NC: University of North Carolina Press, 1944).

19. For example, see UN Charter, Art. 2.4 (1945) ("All Members shall refrain in their international relations from the threat or use of force against the territorial integrity or political independence of any state, or in any other manner inconsistent with the Purposes of the United Nations."). ICJ Statute, Art. 38 sets forth the four sources of international law. Statute of the International Court of Justice Art. 38(1), June 26, 1945, 59 Stat. 1055, 1060, 33 UNTS 933.

20. Rosalyn Higgins, *Problems and Process: International Law and How We Use It* (Oxford: Oxford University Press, 1994), p. 39 ("States are, at this moment of history, still at the heart of the international legal system"). Louis Henkin, *How Nations Behave: Law and Foreign Policy* (New York: Columbia University Press, 1979), p. 40. "That nations are the actors, the legislators, the executives, the judges of international law has led some international lawyers to see law not in terms of norms, standards, and obligations, but as a 'policy-oriented,' comprehensive process of authoritative decision" made largely by the nations themselves." L. Oppenheim, *International Law: A Treatise* (London: Longman, 1905), p. 1 n18.

21. Higgins, *Problems and Process*, p. 1. Aspremont, *International Law as a Belief* System; Mary Ellen O'Connell, *The Art of Law in the International Community* (Cambridge: Cambridge University Press, 2019).

22. Henry M. Hart and Albert M. Sacks, *The Legal Process: Basic Problems in the Making and Application of Law*, William Eskridge Jr. and

Philip Frickey, eds. (New York: Foundation Press, 1994). See Chapter 3 for additional explanation and coverage of legal process theory and international legal process theory.

23. Higgins, p. 2.
24. Oppenheim, *International Law*; Lauterpacht, *The Function of Law*; Phillip Jessup, *Transnational Law* (New Haven, CT: Yale University Press, 1956); Myres McDougal, "International Law, Power and Policy: A Contemporary Conception," *Recueil des Cours: Collected Courses of The Hague Academy of International Law* 82 (1953), 137; Stephen Schwebel, *The Effectiveness of International Decision* (Dobbs Ferry, NY: Oceana Publications, 1971).
25. *Merriam-Webster*, s.v. "choice (*n.*)," accessed December 19, 2019, www .merriam-webster.com/dictionary/choice "the act of choosing or the right or ability to choose."
26. "Realist accounts of international relations scholarship have implicitly, or even explicitly, used rational choice assumptions in order to explain and predict states' behavior: states pursue power rationally." Anne van Aaken, Rational Choice Theory, Oxford Bibliographies (2015), www .oxfordbibliographies.com/view/document/obo-9780199796953/ob o-9780199796953–0051.xml

2 INTERNATIONAL LAW AS HUMAN CHOICE

1. Albert Einstein, *The World as I See It* (trans. by Alan Harris), abridged ed. (New York: Philosophical Library, 1949), p. 63.
2. ICJ Declaration of President Bedjaoui, www.icj-cij.org/files/case-related/9 5/095–19960708-ADV-01–01-EN.pdf.
3. Pursuant to the UN Charter Art. 96, para. 1. UN General Assembly, Request for an Advisory Opinion by the ICJ on the Legality of the Threat or Use of Nuclear Weapons, Res. 49/75, Dec. 15, 1994, www.icj-cij.org/files/ case-related/95/7646.pdf. Boisson de Chazournes and Sands (1991) at p. 4 ("The Resolution was adopted in the face of stiff opposition from many industrialised states, some indicating that they considered the request to be *ultra vires* as it addressed an issue which lay beyond the WHO's competence"). As early as 1961, the United Nations General Assembly and, later, the Security Council reached resolutions laying down political views on nuclear weapons. By 1991, the General Assembly, comprised of representatives from almost every country in the world, determined that using nuclear weapons would constitute a crime against humanity and would violate the terms of the UN Charter. UNGA Resolutions 1653, Nov. 24, 1961; 33/71 B Dec. 14, 1978; 34/83 G Dec. 11, 1979; 25/152 D Dec. 12, 1980; 36/92 I Dec. 9, 1981; 45/59 B Dec. 4, 1990; 46/37 D Dec. 6, 1991.
4. *Guardian*, July 9, 1996; *The Times*, July 9, 1996.

5. ICJ Judgment p. 6, Advisory Opinion on the Legality of the Threat or Use of Nuclear Weapons. ICJ Summary, The Legality of the Threat or Use of Nuclear Weapons, Jul. 8, 1996, www.icj-cij.org/files/case-related/95/7497 .pdf. This advisory opinion, while not binding on states, certainly informs understandings of international law in this area. ICJ Statute Art. 38 "subject to the provisions of Article 59, judicial decisions and the teachings of the most highly qualified publicists of the various nations, as subsidiary means for the determination of rules of law." www.icj-cij.org/en/statute.

6. See the account of John Burroughs, Looking Back: The 1996 Advisory Opinion of the International Court of Justice, 2016, www.armscontrol.org/ ACT/2016_07/Features/Looking-Back-The-1996-Advisory-Opinion-of-th e-International-Court-of-Justice.

7. ICJ Judgment p. 8, Advisory Opinion on the Legality of the Threat or Use of Nuclear Weapons.

8. www.armscontrol.org/ACT/2016_07/Features/Looking-Back-The-1996-Advisory-Opinion-of-the-International-Court-of-Justice.

9. www.icj-cij.org/en/case/95/advisory-opinions.

10. Declaration of Judge Herczegh, p. 275 ("In my view, however, in the present state of international law it would have been possible to formulate in the Advisory Opinion a more specific reply to the General Assembly's request"), www.icj-cij.org/files/case-related/95/095–19960708-ADV-01-02-EN.pdf.

11. Dissenting Opinion of Judge Oda, www.icj-cij.org/files/case-related/95/o 95–19960708-ADV-01-10-EN.pdf.

12. Dissenting Opinion, Judge Rosalyn Higgins, www.icj-cij.org/files/case-related/95/095–19960708-ADV-01-14-EN.pdf, para. 18.

13. Dissenting Opinion of Vice President Schwebel, p. 311, www.icj-cij.org/f iles/case-related/95/095–19960708-ADV-01-09-EN.pdf.

14. For a list of all of these declarations and opinions, see ICJ Advisory Opinion of the Legality of the Threat or Use of Nuclear Weapons, Jul. 8, 1996, www.icj-cij.org/en/case/95/advisory-opinions.

15. ICJ Advisory Opinion of the Legality of the Threat or Use of Nuclear Weapons, Jul. 8, 1996, p. 266, www.icj-cij.org/files/case-related/95/095–19960708-ADV-01–00-EN.pdf. In favor: President Bedjaoui; judges Ranjeva, Herczegh, Shi, Fleischhauer, Vereshchetin, Ferrari Bravo; against: Vice President Schwebel; judges Oda, Guillaume, Shahabuddeen, Weeramantry, Koroma, Higgins.

16. ICJ Statute, Art. 55. 2, "In the event of an equality of votes, the President or the judge who acts in his place shall have a casting vote."

17. ICJ Advisory Opinion the Legality of the Threat or Use of Nuclear Weapons, Jul. 8, 1996, p. 266, www.icj-cij.org/files/case-related/95/095–19960708-ADV -01-00-EN.pdf ("It follows from the above-mentioned requirements that the threat or use of nuclear weapons would generally be contrary to the rules of international law applicable in armed conflict, and in particular the

principles and rules of humanitarian law; However, in view of the current state of international law, and of the elements of fact at its disposal, the Court cannot conclude definitely whether the threat or use of nuclear weapons would be lawful or unlawful in an extreme circumstance of self-defence, in which the very survival of a State would be at stake.").

18. For an authoritative description of the proceedings and views before the court, see Boisson de Chazournes and Sands (1999), pp. 10–23.

19. Susan Butler, *Roosevelt and Stalin* (New York: Knopf, 2015), p. 497. Japan surrendered to Allied Forces on Aug. 15, 1945 and signed the surrender documents on Sept. 2, 1945.

20. The official death tolls were conservative. An estimated 150,000 people were killed instantly in Hiroshima and an estimated 75,000 in Nagasaki. www.aasc.ucla.edu/cab/200708230009.html.

21. Death estimates based on eyewitness reports for Hiroshima are between 90,000–120,000 and for Nagasaki are between 60,000–80,000, www.aasc.ucla.edu/cab/200708230009.html.

22. Japanese Declaration.

23. Oct. 9, 1941.

24. "Notes of Meeting of the Interim Committee, June 1, 1945." The Harry S. Truman Library and Museum. pp. 8–9. Ham, p. 239. (Bard later changed his mind and sent a memo to Stimson urging him to warn Japan before using the bomb. Stimson made the same recommendation on July 17 to Byrnes: warn Japan of the bomb beforehand and assure them that the emperor could remain after the war. Byrnes did not agree.)

25. "The opinions of our scientific colleagues on the initial use of these weapons are not unanimous: they range from the proposal of a purely technical demonstration to that of the military application best designed to induce surrender. Those who advocate a purely technical demonstration would wish to outlaw the use of atomic weapons, and have feared that if we use the weapons now our position in future negotiations will be prejudiced. Others emphasize the opportunity of saving American lives by immediate military use, and believe that such use will improve the international prospects, in that they are more concerned with the prevention of war than with the elimination of this specific weapon. We find ourselves closer to these latter views; we can propose no technical demonstration likely to bring an end to the war; we see no acceptable alternative to direct military use." Notes of Meeting of the Interim Committee.

26. *Ibid.*

27. Ham, p. 225.

28. Declassified Top Secret notes on Initial Meeting of Target Committee (May, 1945).

29. Declassified Top Secret Memo detailing the information on Kyoto and its desirability as a target (Jul. 2, 1945). Ham, p. 148 (noting that the target

should "be mostly intact, to demonstrate the awesome destructive power of an atomic bomb").

30. Declassified Top Secret Memo on Kyoto (Jul. 2, 1945) identifying it as a "[t]ypical Jap city" and identifying universities, colleges and cultural areas as targets.

31. For context, see Sean L. Malloy, *Atomic Tragedy: Henry L. Stimson and the Decision to Use the Bomb Against Japan* (Ithaca, NY: NYU Press, 2008); Sean Malloy, "Four Days in May: Henry L. Stimson and the Decision to Use the Atomic Bomb," *Asia-Pacific Journal*, 7, issue 14, no. 2 (Apr. 4, 2009).

32. Declassified, Top Secret Memo, From Chief of Staff, Twentieth Air-Force to Director, Join Target Group (Apr. 28, 1945). Ham, p. 148.

33. Ham, p. 152.

34. Telecon Message, DC/S Combat Operation (Jun., 27 1945). Ham, p. 67.

35. Ham, p. 241.

36. Malloy, "Four Days in May"; Jason M. Kelly, "Why Did Henry Stimson Spare Kyoto from the Bomb? Confusion in Postwar Historiography," 19 *Journal of American-East Relations* (2012), 183–203.

37. Henry Stimson, "The Decision to Use the Atomic Bomb" *Harper's* (Feb., 1947), 97–107; Stimson Diary, "Memorandum for the President: Proposed Program for Japan" (Jul. 2, 1945).

38. "Dear Dick, I know that Japan is a terribly cruel and uncivilized nation in warfare but I can't bring myself to believe that, because they are beasts, we should ourselves act in the same manner. For myself I certainly regret the necessity of wiping out whole populations because of the 'pigheadedness' of the leaders of a nation and, for your information, I am not going to do it unless it is absolutely necessary. It is my opinion that after the Russians enter into the war the Japanese will very shortly fold up. My objective is to save as many American lives as possible but I also have a human feeling for the women and children of Japan. Sincerely yours, Harry S. Truman". Letter Harry S. Truman to Richard Russell, Aug. 9, 1945, Harry S. Truman Library, www.trumanlibrary.gov/library/research-files/harry-s-truman-richard-russell.

39. Henry Stimson, US Secretary of War, *Harper's Magazine*, Feb., 1947.

40. UN Charter (1945), www.un.org/en/charter-united-nations/.

41. Fifty nations signed the UN Charter at the San Francisco Conference on October 24, 1945. Constructed during the war by US President Roosevelt, UK Prime Minister Churchill and Soviet Premier Josef Stalin, the UN Charter would be led by five nations or "policemen" to enforce the rules: America, China, France, Russia, and the United Kingdom (in their modern names). See United Nations, History of the United Nations, www.un.org/en/sections/history/history-united-nations/. For a history of these events, see Diana Preston, *Eight Days at Yalta* (London: Picador, 2019).

42. ICJ Declaration of President Bedjaoui, www.icj-cij.org/files/case-related /95/095–19960708-ADV-01–01-EN.pdf.

43. For a helpful overview of theories of international law, see Anne Orford and Florian Hoffman, eds., *The Oxford Handbook of the Theory of International Law* (Oxford: Oxford University Press, 2016); Oona A. Hathaway and Harold Hongju Koh, *Foundations of International Law and Politics* (New York: Foundation Press, 2005).

44. For critical race theory scholarship, see Kimberlé Williams Crenshaw, *Critical Race Theory: The Key Writings that Formed the Movement* (New York: New Press, 1996); Angela Harris, foreword to Richard Delgado and Jean Stefancic, *Critical Race Theory: An Introduction*, 3rd ed. (New York: NYU Press, 2017); Athena D. Mutua, "The Rise, Development, and Future Directions of Critical Race Theory and Related Scholarship," *Denver University Law Review* 84, no. 2 (2006); Angela Onwuachi-Willig, "Celebrating Critical Race Theory at 20," *Iowa Law Review* 94, no. 5 (2009). For critical race feminism, see Adrien Wing, *Critical Race Feminism* (New York: NYU Press, 2003). For TWAIL, see Balakrishnan Rajagopal, *International Law from Below: Development, Social Movements and Third World Resistance* (Cambridge: Cambridge University Press, 2003); Antony Anghie, *Imperialism, Sovereignty and the Making of International Law* (Cambridge: Cambridge University Press, 2005); Makau Mutua, *Human Rights Standards: Hegemony, Law and Politics* (Albany, NY: State University of New York Press, 2016); James Thuo Gathii, "Writing Race and Identity in a Global Context: What CRT and TWAIL Can Learn From Each Other," 67 *UCLA Law Review* (2020).

45. See Henry M. Hart and Albert M. Sacks, *The Legal Process: Basic Problems in the Making and Application of Law*, eds. William Eskridge Jr. and Philip Frickey (New York: Foundation Press, 1994), p. liii (explaining that legal process theory "went well beyond the traditional law story" to describe law as "essential to the satisfaction of basic human wants and needs and to the advancement of humankind").

46. "[A] procedure which is soundly adapted to the type of power to be exercised is conducive to well-informed and wise decisions. An unsound procedure invites ill-informed and unwise ones." Hart and Sacks, *The Legal Process*, p. xciv. "[L]aw comprises (although it may not be confined to) a series of institutionalized processes for settling by authority of the group various types of questions of concern to the group." Henry M. Hart, *Note on Some Essential of a Working Theory of Law* (Hart Papers, Harvard University Library, Box 1, Folder 1, 1950). Regarding one such process, adjudication, see Lon L. Fuller, "The Forms and Limits of Adjudication," *Harvard Law Review* 92, no. 2 (1978), 354 (defining adjudication to include "adjudicative bodies which owe their powers to the consent of

the litigants expressed in an agreement of submission, as in labor relations and in international law").

47. Harold D. Lasswell and Myres Smith McDougal, *Jurisprudence for a Free Society* (New Haven, CT: New Haven Press, 1992), p. xxi. See also Myres S. McDougal, "Law and Power," *American Journal of International Law* 46 (1952), 108–9 (arguing that people identify and demand values "that transcend national boundaries because they have come to know that the conditions under which they can secure their values transcend such boundaries," that in order to obtain these values they organize institutions that range from governments to political parties and private associations, and that "[d]ecisions which affect the world distribution of power and other values are made at all points in this complicated matrix of inter-related institutions"); Michael Reisman, "The New Haven School: A Brief Introduction," *Yale Journal of International Law* 32, no. 2 (2007)("The New Haven School's policy-oriented jurisprudence sketched an anti-formalist concept of law tailored to concerns of international justice understood in an individualistic way"); Eisuke Suzuki, The New Haven School of International Law: An Invitation to a Policy-Oriented Jurisprudence, 1 Yale J. World Pub. Ord. 1, 30 (1974).

48. Abram Chayes, Thomas Ehlrich, and Andreas F. Lowenfeld, *International Legal Process* (Boston: Little, Brown, & Company, 1968), pp. xiv, xi (establishing a focus on "the study of the international legal process itself" and noting that "[f]or an adequate understanding of the norm we need to see ... by what institutions and procedures it is brought to bear in particular cases"). Steven R. Ratner and Anne-Marie Slaughter, "Appraising the Methods of International Law: A Prospectus for Readers," in *The Methods of International Law*, eds. Anne-Marie Slaughter and Steven Ratner (Washington, DC: American Society of International Law, 2004), p. 6 (noting international legal process as developed by Chayes, Erlich, and Lowenfeld "has seen the key locus of inquiry of international law as the role of law in constraining decision makers and affecting the course of international affairs").

49. See Chayes, Ehlrich, and Lowenfeld, *International Legal Process*, p. xi (asking "[h]ow – and how far – do law, lawyers, and legal institutions operate to affect the course of international affairs?").

50. See Abram Chayes and Antonia Handler Chayes, *The New Sovereignty: Compliance with International Regulatory Agreements* (Cambridge, MA: Harvard University Press, 1998).

51. See Harold H. Koh, "Transnational Legal Process," *Nebraska Law Review* 75, no. 1 (1996), 183–4 (explaining transnational legal process as describing "the theory and practice of how public and private actors ... interact in a variety of public and private, domestic and

international fora to make, interpret, enforce, and ultimately, internalize rules of transnational law").

52. See, for example, Louis Henkin, *Why Nations Behave* (1979); Thomas Franck, *The Power of Legitimacy Among Nations* (Oxford: Oxford University Press, 1990), 50–1 (taking a process-based, norm-centered approach to understanding rule legitimacy).

53. See Mary Ellen O'Connell, "New International Legal Process," in *The Methods of International Law*, eds. Anne-Marie Slaughter and Steven Ratner (Washington, DC: American Society of International Law, 2004), pp. 85–6 (discussing the emergence of the NILP approach, with an "agenda ... to balance form and substance, to view the legal system as a purposive whole, and to explore both functionally and formally institutional competence and the role of process"); Koh, "Transnational Legal Process," (describing the critical reaction to the legal process movement that "viewed lawmaking as not merely the rubberstamping of a pluralistic political process, but as a process of value-creation in which the courts, agencies, and the people engage in a process of democratic dialogue").

54. For a description of the NILP approach in international law, see Slaughter and Ratner, "Appraising the Methods of International Law," 256.

55. These include economics, psychology, mathematics, sociology, behavioral science, and more. Note that each discipline defines choice in its own way and there is no generally accepted framework for comparing the research or insights among or between these fields. For a classic overview of thinking about decision making in law, see Paul Brest and Linda Hamilton Krieger, *Problems Solving Decision Making and Professional Judgment* (New York: Oxford University Press, 2010), p. 366 ("People are in principle capable of pursuing their ends – whatever they may be – in a rational manner").

56. "The core premise of economic theory is that people choose by optimizing." "The premise of constrained optimization, that is, choosing the best from a limited budget, is combined with the other major workhorse of economic theory, that of equilibrium ... . To simplify somewhat, we can say that Optimization + Equilibrium = Economics." Thaler, *Misbehaving*, p. 5. See Adam Smith, *The Theory of Moral Sentiments*, eds. D.D. Raphael and A.L. Macfie (Indianapolis, IN: Liberty Classics, 1981) (discussing the sentiments, emotions, and passions underlying human nature and predating his magnum opus, *The Wealth of Nations* (1776)).

57. See early work from the 1950s, including Leonard Jimmie Savage, *The Foundations of Statistics* (Hoboken, NJ: John Wiley & Sons, 1954); R. Duncan Luce and Howard Raiffa, *Games and Decisions:*

Introduction and Critical Survey (New York: Wiley, 1957). More recent works include Stephen R. Watson and Dennis M. Buede, *Decision Synthesis: The Principles and Practice of Decision Analysis* (Cambridge: Cambridge University Press, 1987); Robert T. Clemen, *Making Hard Decisions: An Introduction to Decision Analysis,* 2nd ed. (Belmont, CA: Duxbury Press, 1996) (explaining model-oriented decision analysis in business context); Peter McNamee and John Celona, *Decision Analysis for the Professional,* 4th ed. (New York: Smartorg, Inc., 2001); R.L. Keeney and Howard Raiffa, *Decisions with Multiple Objectives: Preferences and Value Tradeoffs* (Cambridge: Cambridge University Press, 1993); Rex Brown, *Rational Choice and Judgment: Decision Analysis for the Decider* (Hoboken, NJ: Wiley-Interscience, 2005).

58. Brown, *Rational Choice and Judgment,* pp. xviii, xv. Noting the need to focus on "real decisionmakers" Brown argues: "In order to outperform an unaided decider, DA needs not only to be logically sound, but also to take full account of the decider's human and institutional requirements and to draw on all of his/her knowledge."

59. Irving L. Janis, *Groupthink: Psychological Studies of Foreign Policy Decisions and Fiascos* (New York: Houghton-Mifflin, 1982) (setting forth the argument that the quality of the decision-making process influence the quality of the decisions made in the foreign policy context); Paul 't Hart, Eric K. Stern, and Bengt Sundelius, eds., *Beyond Groupthink: Political Dynamics and Foreign Policy-Making* (Ann Arbor, MI: University of Michigan Press, 1997); Dominic Johnson, *Overconfidence and War: The Havoc and Glory of Positive Illusions* (Cambridge, MA: Harvard University Press, 2004), p. 5 (arguing that overconfidence is an adaptive trait of human evolutionary biology and contributes to causing war); Gregory M. Herek, Irving L. Janis, and Paul Huth, "Decision Making During International Crises," *Journal of Conflict Resolution* 31, no. 2 (1987), 203–4 (explaining why rational choice theory is descriptively and normatively inadequate for improving the quality of decisions); Alex Mintz and Carly Wayne, *The Polythink Syndrome: U.S. Foreign Policy Decisions on 9/11, Afghanistan, Iraq, Iran, Syria, and ISIS* (Stanford, CA: Stanford University Press, 2016), p. 3 (describing ways in which "rational decision makers engage in flawed decision-making process that deeply affect the security and welfare of a country").

60. Robert O. Keohane, "Rational Choice Theory and International Law: Insights and Limitations," *Journal of Legal Studies* 31, no. S1 (2002), S310. According to Jon Elster: "An action to be rational, must be the final result of three optimal decisions. First, it must be the best means of realizing an individual's desires, given his beliefs. Next, these beliefs must themselves be optimal, given the information available to him. Finally, the person

must collect an optimal amount of evidence – neither too much nor too little." Jon Elster, *Nuts and Bolts for the Social Sciences* (Cambridge: Cambridge University Press, 1989), p. 30. Such models offer hypotheses for human behavior under certain conditions but are not conclusive or comprehensive. Keohane, "Rational Choice Theory and International Law," S308–S309.

61. Gary King, Robert O. Keohane, and Sidney Verba, *Designing Social Inquiry: Scientific Inference in Qualitative Research* (Princeton, NJ: Princeton University Press, 1994).

62. Keohane, "Rational Choice Theory and International Law," S307.

63. Stephen D. Krasner, "Structural Causes and Regime Consequences: Regimes as Intervening Variables," in *International Regimes*, ed. Stephen D. Krasner (Ithaca, NY: Cornell University Press, 1983); Kenneth W. Abbott, "Modern International Relations Theory: A Prospectus for International Lawyers," *Yale Journal of International Law* 14, no. 2 (1989); Anne-Marie Slaughter Burley, "International Law and International Relations Theory: A Dual Agenda," *American Journal of International Law* 87, no. 2 (1993), 220; Kenneth W. Abbott and Duncan Snidal, "Hard and Soft Law in International Governance," in *Legalization and World Politics*, ed. Goldstein et al. (Boston, MA: MIT Press, 2001), p. 37; Alan O. Sykes and Warren F. Schwartz, "Economic Structure of Renegotiation and Dispute Resolution in the World Trade Organization, The Rational Choice and International Law," *Journal of Legal Studies* 31 (2002), S170; Zachary Elkins, Andrew T. Guzman, and Beth A. Simmons, "Competing for Capital: The Diffusion of Bilateral Investment Treaties, 1960–2000" *International Organization* 60 (2008), 811–46.

64. Kenneth Abbot and Duncan Snidal, "Values and Interests: International Legalization in the Fight Against Corruption," *Journal of Legal Studies* 31, no. S1 (2002).

65. See, for example, Cass R. Sunstein, ed., *Behavioral Law and Economics* (New York: Cambridge University Press, 2000); Jolls, Sunstein and Thaler, "A Behavioral Approach to Law and Economics"; Christine Jolls and Cass R. Sunstein , "Debiasing Through Law," *Journal of Legal Studies* 35, no. 1 (2006); Anne van Aaken, "Towards Behavioral International Law and Economics: A Comment on Enriching Rational Choice Institutionalism for the Study of International Law," *University of Illinois Law Review*, 2008, no. 1 (2008), 60.

66. Daniel Kahneman and Amos Tversky, ed., *Choices, Values, and Frames* (Cambridge: Cambridge University Press, 2000); Daniel Kahneman, *Thinking Fast and Slow* (New York: Farrar, Straus, & Giroux, 2011). Hogarth and Reder, *Rational Choice*.

67. "It is time to stop making excuses. We need an enriched approach to doing economic research, one that acknowledges the existence and relevance of Humans." Thaler, *Misbehaving*, pp. 6–7.

68. Amos Tverskey and Daniel Kahneman, "Judgment Under Uncertainty: Heuristics and Biases," *in Judgment Under Uncertainty: Heuristics and Biases*, eds. Daniel Kahneman, Paul Slovic, and Amos Tversky (Cambridge: Cambridge University Press, 1982), 3 (explaining that the processes that individuals use to make decisions can sometimes lead to "severe and systematic errors"). For examples in various contexts, see Cass R. Sunstein and Richard H. Thaler, "Libertarian Paternalism Is Not an Oxymoron," *University of Chicago Law Review*, 70, no. 4 (2003), 1167–70 (arguing humans will commonly make decisions contrary to their own interests); Herek, Janis, and Huth, "Decision Making During International Crises," 204 (explaining why rational choice theory is descriptively and normatively inadequate for improving the quality of decisions); Oren Bar-Gill, *Seduction by Contract: Law, Economics, and Psychology in Consumer Markets* (Oxford: Oxford University Press, 2012), p. 2; George A. Akerlof and Robert J. Shiller, *Phishing for Phools: The Economics of Manipulation and Deception* (Princeton, NJ: Princeton University Press, 2015), pp. 6–7 (explaining how marketers use well-known psychological principles to encourage customers to make purchases contrary to their best interests).

69. Johnson, *Overconfidence and War*, p. 6 (describing adaptive overconfidence as a widespread human trait; for examples, studies suggest that people who use more positive words than negative in their daily vocabulary recall positive memories more readily than negative ones, tend to be overly optimistic about the future, and are more likely to evaluate themselves more positively than others).

70. Johnson, *Overconfidence and War*, p. 6 (providing positive and negative examples of overconfidence).

71. See, for example, Luciana Carraro et al., "Implicit and Explicit Illusory Correlation as a Function of Political Identity," *PLOS ONE* 9, no. 5 (2014), www.ncbi.nlm.nih.gov/pmc/articles/PMC4018394/pdf/pone .0096312.pdf [https://perma.cc/VPC6-5NCQ] ("Illusory correlation is the tendency to misperceive the covariation between two events, and, more specifically, the tendency to believe that two relatively infrequent events are associated with each other even though no such association is actually present").

72. Rob Henderson, "How Powerful Is Status Quo Bias?" *Psychology Today*, September 29, 2016, www.psychologytoday.com/blog/after-service/20160 9/how-powerful-is-status-quo-bias [https://perma.cc/Q34Z-KHNP].

73. Tversky and Kahneman, *Judgment Under Uncertainty*, 14–8 (describing anchoring).

74. Tversky and Kahneman, *Judgment Under Uncertainty*, 79–88 (describing heuristics as a "machine for jumping to conclusions" that lead to overconfidence, framing effects, base-rate neglect, and other cognitive biases).

75. Herbert Simon, *Models of Man: Social and Rational* (Hoboken, NJ: John Wiley & Sons, 1957), pp. 204–5. See also Shelley E. Taylor, "The Availability Bias in Social Perception and Interaction," in Tversky and Kahneman, *Judgment Under Uncertainty*, 190–1 (explaining the meaning of "satisfice").

76. See Simon, *Models of Man*, p. 256 (explaining the difference in rational decision-making ability between the "economic man" and a "choosing individual of limited knowledge and ability").

77. See, for example, Rosalind Dixon and Tom Ginsburg, "Deciding Not to Decide: Deferral in Constitutional Design," *International Journal of Constitutional Law* 9, no. 3–4 (2011), 639 ("When the stakes are high, there is naturally some reluctance to making the wrong decision too early; when stakes are low but the probability of error is high, deferral also makes sense as a strategy").

78. Kahan, "Laws of Cognition and the Cognition of Law," 56 ("[l]aw and particularly adjudication have historically been a vibrant site for the study of cognition ... [as] adjudication furnishes a consequential, real-world decision-making system, the relative simplicity of which supports experimental designs that isolate mechanisms of interest from confounds without (it is hoped) compromising external validity."); Rose McDermott, "New Directions for Experimental Work in International Relations," *International Studies Quarterly* 55, no. 2 (2011); Emilie M. Hafner-Burton et al., "The Behavioral Revolution and International Relations," *International Organization* 71, Supplement (2017); Susan D. Franck, *Arbitration Costs: Myths and Realities in Investment Treaty Arbitration* (Oxford: Oxford University Press, 2019), pp. 25–66 (discussing the use of insights from cognitive psychology, including cognitive illusions and biases, on international treaty arbitration); *International Law as Behavior* (2020).

79. See, for example, Gregory Shaffer and Tom Ginsburg "The Empirical Turn in International Legal Scholarship," *American Journal of International Law* 106, no. 1 (2016); Susan Franck et al., "Inside the Arbitrator's Mind," *Emory Law Journal* 66, no. 5 (2017), 1115–18 (describing its "experimental method"); Rebecca Helm, Andrew J. Wistrich, and Jeffrey J. Rachlinski, "Are Arbitrators Human?" *Journal of Empirical Legal Studies* 13, no. 4 (2016), 669–70 (suggesting that "arbitrators lack an inherent advantage over judges when it comes to making high-quality decisions"); Sophie Nappert and Dieter Flader,

"Psychological Factors in the Arbitral Process," in *The Art of Advocacy in International Arbitration*, Doak Bishop and Edward G. Kehoe eds., 2nd ed. (Juris Net, 2010) (surveying international arbitrators on aspects of persuasion and receiving a low response rate of nineteen responses). Donald C. Langevoort, "Behavioral Theories of Judgment and Decision Making in Legal Scholarship: A Literature Review," *Vanderbilt Law Review* 51, no. 6 (1998). See also Christine Jolls, Cass R. Sunstein, and Richard Thaler, "A Behavioral Approach to Law and Economics," *Stanford Law Review* 50, no. 5 (1998). See, for example, Amos Tversky and Daniel Kahnemann, "Rational Choice and the Framing of Decisions," in *Rational Choice: The Contrast Between Economics and Psychology*, Robin M. Hogarth and Melvin W. Reder eds. (Chicago, IL: University of Chicago Press, 1987).

80. Declaration of Bedjaoi, pp. 269–70.

81. Separate Opinion of Judge Guillaume, p. 293, www.icj-cij.org/files/case-related/95/095-19960708-ADV-01-06-EN.pdf.

82. Higgins, *Problems and Processes*, 1. "International law is not rules. It is a normative system." Rosalyn Higgins, "General Course on Public International Law," Recueil des Cours 230 (1991), 23 (H.L.A. Hart, *The Concept of Law* (Oxford: Oxford University Press, 1961), p. 84 ("[r]ules are conceived and spoken of as imposing obligations when the general demand for conformity is insistent and the social pressure brought to bear upon those who deviate or threaten to deviate is great").

83. "[I]nternational law bears the attributes of a belief system." Jean d'Aspremont, *International Law as a Belief System* (Cambridge: Cambridge University Press, 2018), p. 3.

84. "When ... decisions are made by authorized persons or organs, in appropriate forums, within the framework of certain established practices and norms, then what occurs is *legal* decision-making. In other words, international law is a continuing process of authoritative decisions. This view rejects the notion of law as merely the impartial applications of rules." Higgins, *Problems and Processes*, p. 2, citing Higgins, "Policy Considerations," 58–9.

85. Higgins, Problems and Process, p. 2.

86. Higgins, p. 3.

87. Hersch Lauterpacht, *The Development of International Law by the International Court* (1958).

88. "These principle decisionmakers, filling more or less parallel roles in the 'world power process,' include international governmental organizations, transnational political parties and pressure groups, private associations, and individual human beings, along with nations states themselves." Stone, *Visions of World Order*, pp. 22–3.

3 HOW PEOPLE CHOOSE

1. Richard Thaler, *Misbehaving: The Making of Behavioral Economics* (New York: W.W. Norton & Company, 2015), p. 355.
2. *Merriam-Webster*, s.v. "choice (*n.*)," accessed July 20, 2020, www.merriam-webster.com/dictionary/choice ("the act of choosing").
3. *Merriam-Webster*, s.v. "decision (n.)" accessed July 20, 2020, www.merriam-webster.com/dictionary/decision ("the act or process of deciding").
4. Michael S. Gazzaniga , Richard Ivry, and George Mangun, 3rd ed. (2008) (providing a general overview of the field); Cognitive Neuroscience: The Biology of the Mind, James Schwartz et al., Principles of Neural Science, 5th ed. (2013); The Cambridge Handbook of Human Affective Neuroscience 1, Jorge Armony and Patrik Vuilleumier eds. (2013). *Handbook of Emotion Regulation*, James J. Gross, ed. (New York: Guilford Press, 2007). For recent works in this area, see Russell A. Poldrack, *The New Mind Readers: What Neuroimaging Can and Cannot Reveal about Our Thoughts* (Princeton, NJ: Princeton University Press, 2018); Ralph Adolphs and David J. Anderson, *The Neuroscience of Emotion: A New Synthesis* (Princeton, NJ: Princeton University Press, 2018); Kevin J. Mitchell, *Innate: How the Wiring of Our Brains Shapes Who We Are* (Princeton, NJ: Princeton University Press, 2018); A.D. Craig, *How Do You Feel? An Interoceptive Moment with Your Neurobiological Self* (Princeton, NJ: Princeton University Press, 2014).
5. Tara Niendam, A.R. Laird, K.L. Ray, Y.M. Dean, D.C. Glahn, and C. S. Carter, "Meta-Analytic Evidence for a Superordinate Cognitive Control Network Subserving Diverse Executive Functions," *Cognitive, Affective, & Behavioral Neuroscience* (June 12, 2019), 241–68 (providing a meta-analysis of 193 functional neuroimaging studies on 2,832 people performing executive function tasks associated with higher cognition provides evidence that cognitive activity took place throughout the brain in the dorsolateral prefrontal, dorsal anterior cingulate, parietal cortices – frontoparietal network).
6. For a recent example and explanation see "How the Brain Makes Choices," *The Conversation, Neuroscience News*, accessed January 11, 2019, http://neurosciencenews.com/brain-choices-11504/.
7. Such as the well-known practice of seeking out information that affirms past choices, otherwise known as confirmation bias. Dan Ariely, *Predictably Irrational: The Hidden Forces That Shape Our Decisions*, rev. and expanded ed. (HarperCollins, 2009). See, generally, Kahneman, *Thinking Fast and Slow*; Thaler and Sunstein, *Nudge*, 66 (claiming that desirable behavior can be increased by drawing public attention to what others are doing); Thaler, *Misbehaving*.

8. Vartanian and Mandel, *The Neuroscience of Decision Making*, p. 2.
9. Vartanian and Mandel, p. 2.
10. Vartanian and Mandel, p. 2. Antoine Bechara, "Human Emotions in Decision Making: Are They Useful or Disruptive?" in *The Neuroscience of Decision Making*, eds. Oshin Vartanian and Dave R. Mandel (New York: Psychology Press, 2011), pp. 73, 74, 76 ("This mechanism for selecting good from bad options is referred to as decision making, and the physiological changes occurring in association with the behavior selection constitute part of somatic states (or somatic signals)").
11. Michael Kosfeld et al., "Oxytocin Increases Trust in Humans," *Nature* 435, 2 (2005), 673–5.
12. Leslie Fellows, "The Neuroscience of Human Decision-Making Through the Lens of Learning and Memory," in *Current Topics in Behavioral Neurosciences*, eds. Robert E. Clark and Stephen Martin (New York: Springer International Publishing, 2018), pp. 37, 231.
13. Vartanian and Mandel, *The Neuroscience of Decision Making*, p. 2.
14. Brian Knutson et al., "Distributed Neural Representation of Expected Value," *Journal of Neuroscience* 25, no. 19 (2005), 4806; John P. O'Doherty and Peter Bossaerts , "Toward a Mechanistic Understanding of Human Decision Making: Contributions of Functional Neuroimaging," *Current Directions Psychological Science* 17, no. 2 (2008), 119–23.
15. C.H. Salmond, D.K. Menon, D.A. Chatfield, J.D. Pickard, and B. J. Sahakian, "Deficits in Decision-Making in Head Injury Survivors," 22 *Journal of Neurotrauma* 613–22 (2005); https://pubmed.ncbi.nlm.nih.gov /15941371/.
16. Nathalie Camille, Ami Tsuchida, and Lesley K. Fellows, "Double Dissociation of Stimulus-Value and Action-Value Learning in Humans with Orbitofrontal or Anterior Cingulate Cortex Damage," *Journal of Neuroscience* 31 (2011). See also, McGill University "Decision-Making: What You Want vs. How You Get It," *Science Daily*, October 23, 2011.
17. Akram Bakkour, Daniela J. Palombo, Ariel Zylberberg, Yul H.R. Kang, Allison Reid, Mieke Verfaellie, Michael N. Shadlen, and Daphna Shohamy, "The Hippocampus Supports Deliberation during Value-Based Decisions," *ELife*, Jul. 3, 2019.
18. For a description of cognitive errors, see Joachim I. Krueger and David C. Funder, "Toward a Balanced Social Psychology," *Behav. & Brain Science* 27 (2007), 313, 317.
19. The Selective Attention Test, www.youtube.com/watch?v=_bnnmWYIolM. Christopher Chabris and Daniel Simons, *The Invisible Gorilla: How Our Intentions Deceive Us* (New York: Broadway Paperbacks, 2009). Daniel

J. Simons and Daniel T. Levin, "Failure to Detect Changes to People During a Real-World Interaction," *Psychonomic Bull. & Rev* 5, 644 (1998).

20. For international legal scholarship employing behavioral research, see Susan D. Franck, *Arbitration Costs: Myths and Realities in Investment Treaty Arbitration*, (New York: Oxford University Press, 2019); Emilie Hafner-Burton et al., "The Behavioral Revolution and International Relations," *Int'l Org.* 71 (2017): pp. S1–S31; Tomer Broude, "Behavioral International Law," 163 *U. Penn. L. Rev.* 1099 (2015); Ganesh Sitaraman and David Zionts, "Behavioral War Powers," 90 *NYU L. Rev.* 516, 521–523 (2015); Anne van Aaken, "Behavioral International Law and Economics," 55 *Harv. Int'l L. J.* 421 (2014); Jean Galbraith, "Treaty Options: Towards a Behavioral Understanding of Treaty Design," 53 *Va. J. Int'l L.* 309–310, 312, 356 (2013); Andrew K. Woods, "A Behavioral Approach to Human Rights," 51 *Harv. Int'l L. J.* 51 (2010); Anne van Aaken, "Towards Behavioral International Law and Economics," 2008 *U. Ill. L. Rev.* 47 (2008).

21. Dan Ariely, Predictably Irrational. Heuristics and Biases: The Psychology of Intuitive Judgment (Thomas Gilovich, et al., eds., 2002). Robyn M. Dawes, *Everyday Irrationality: How Pseudo-Scientists, Lunatics, and the Rest of US Fail to Think Rationally* (2001). Anuj K. Shah and Daniel M. Oppenheimer, "Heuristics Made Easy: An Effort-Reduction Framework," *Psych. Bull.* 134 (2008), 207.

22. Gary S. Becker, *The Economic Approach to Human Behavior* (Chicago, IL: University of Chicago Press, 1976). For an exploration of decision making models in foreign policy, see, generally, Alex Mintz and Karl DeRouen Jr., *Understanding Foreign Policy Decision Making* (New York: Cambridge University Press, 2010).

23. For sources studying group decision making in the foreign policy arena, see Irving L. Janis, *Groupthink: Psychological Studies of Policy Decisions and Fiascoes* (Boston, MA: Houghton-Mifflin,1982); Paul 't Hart, Eric K. Stern, and Bengt Sundelius, eds., *Beyond Groupthink: Political Group Dynamics and Foreign Policy-Making* (Ann Arbor, MI: University of Michigan Press, 1997).

24. Stephen Morse, "Brain Overclaim Syndrome and Criminal Responsibility: A Diagnostic Note," Ohio State Journal of Criminal Law 3, no. 2 (2006), 397–412; Michael S. Pardo and Dennis Patterson, *Minds, Brains, and Law: The Conceptual Foundations of Law and Neuroscience* (Oxford: Oxford University Press, 2013).

25. See, for example, William Hirstein, Katrina L. Sifferd, and Tyler K. Fagan, *Responsible Brains: Neuroscience, Law, and Human Culpability* (Cambridge, MA: MIT Press, 2018), p. 12 ("Evidence from cognitive science and neuroscience can illuminate and inform the nature of responsibility and agency in specific, testable ways").

26. Spain Bradley, "Advancing Neuroscience in International Law." For recent research at the intersection of law and neuroscience, see Owen D. Jones, Jeffrey D. Schall, and Francis X. Shen, Law and Neuroscience (New York: Wolters Kluwer, 2nd ed. 2020).

27. Kahneman, *Thinking Fast and Slow*.

28. Kahneman, pp. 20–1. See also Tversky and Kahneman, *Judgment Under Uncertainty*, pp. 85–98; Daniel Kahneman, "A Perspective on Judgment and Choice: Mapping Bounded Rationality," *American Psychologist* 58, no. 9 (2003), 698–9 ("The operations of System 1 are typically fast, automatic, effortless, associative, implicit … . [t]he operations of System 2 are slower, serial, effortful, more likely to be consciously monitored and deliberately controlled").

29. Vartanian and Mandel, *The Neuroscience of Decision Making*, p. 2.

30. Vartanian and Mandel, *The Neuroscience of Decision Making*, p. 2.

31. Matar Haller et al., "Persistent Neuronal Activity in Human Prefrontal Cortex Links Perception and Action," *Nature Human Behavior* 2 (2018), 80–91; https://doi.org/10.1038/s41562-017-0267-2.

32. Antoine Bechara et al., "Different Contributions of the Human Amygdala and Ventromedial Prefrontal Cortex to Decision-Making," *Journal of Neuroscience* 19, no. 13 (1999), 5473 (discussing how the ventromedial prefrontal cortex and the amygdala affect different processes).

33. John Anderson et al., "Hidden Stages of Cognition Revealed in Patterns of Brain Activation," *Psycholo. Sci.* 27, 1215 (2016).

34. Kalina Christoff et al., "The Role of Spontaneous Thought in Human Cognition," in *The Neuroscience of Decisionmaking*, Oshin Vartanian and David R. Mandel eds., 2011) (New York: Psychology Press, 2011), pp. 261–3.

35. Christoff et al., 261–3.

36. Akram Bakkour, Daniela J. Palombo, Ariel Zylberberg, Yul H.R. Kang, Allison Reid, Mieke Verfaellie, Michael N. Shadlen, and Daphna Shohamy, The Hippocampus Support Deliberation During Value-Based Decisions, *eLife*, Jul. 3, 2019, https://elifesciences.org/articles/46080.

37. Christoff et al., p. 261.

38. Christoff et al., p. 264 ("These findings suggest that long-term memory processes contribute strongly to the phenomenon of spontaneous thought … memory consolidation may be one of the main functions of spontaneous thought").

39. Christoff et al., p. 264.

40. Darren M. Lipnicki and Don G. Byrne, "Thinking on Your Back: Solving Anagrams Faster When Supine Than When Standing," *Cognitive Brain Research* 24, no. 3 (2005).

41. M. P. Walker et al., "Cognitive Flexibility Across the Sleep-Wake Cycle: REM-sleep Enhancement of Anagram Problem Solving," *Cognitive Brain Research* 14, no. 3 (2002).

42. Peter Graf and Michael E.J. Masson, eds., *Implicit Memory: New Direction in Cognition, Development and Neuropsychology* (New York: Lawrence Erlbaum Associates, Inc., 1993).

43. Aaron M. Nornstein, Mel W. Khaw, Daphna Shohamy, and Nathaniel D. Daw, *Reminders of Past Choices Bias Decisions for Reward in Humans* (Jun. 2017), Nature Communications, https://shohamylab .zuckermaninstitute.columbia.edu/sites/default/files/content/ncomm s15958.pdf

44. Haakon G. Engen and Tania Singer , "Empathy Circuits," *Current Opinion in Neurobiology* 23, no. 2 (2013) ("Empathy can be defined as the process by which an individual infers the affective sate of another by generating an isomorphic affective state in the self, while retaining knowledge that the cause of the affective state is the other"). Daniel Batson, "These Things Called Empathy: Eight Related but Distinct Phenomena," in *The Social Neuroscience of Empathy*, eds. Jean Decety and William Ickes (Cambridge, MA: MIT Press, 2009), p. 11.

45. In other words, there is no single controlling definition of empathy from a neuro-scientific perspective. See Batson, "These Things Called Empathy," pp. 3–15 (describing eight concepts for understanding the phenomenon of one person's caring response to another's suffering).

46. Batson, pp. 3–5.

47. See Frans de Waal, "The Evolution of Empathy," Greater Good Magazine, September 1, 2005, http://greatergood.berkeley.edu/article/ite m/the_evolution_of_empathy (reporting that empathy was critical to survival as a species and summarizing studies performed on animals and other mammals).

48. C. Daniel Batson, "These Things Called Empathy: Eight Related but Distinct Phenomena," in eds. Jean Decety and William Ickes, *The Social Neuroscience of Empathy* pp. 3–11 (2009) (discussing how to define empathy and identifying "eight distinct phenomena that have been called empathy").

49. Anjali Krishnan et al., "Somatic and Vicarious Pain are Represented by Dissociable Multivariate Brain Patterns," *eLife* 5 (2016), 3, http://elifesciences .org/content/5/e15166-download.pdf. See "Empathy for Others' Pain Rooted in Cognition Rather Than Sensation, CU-Boulder Study Finds," *CU Boulder Today*, University of Colorado Boulder, June 14, 2016, www .colorado.edu/today/2016/06/14/empathy-others-pain-rooted-cognition-rather -sensation-cu-boulder-study-finds ("The research suggests that empathy is a deliberative process that requires taking another person's perspective rather than being an instinctive, automatic process.")

50. Jeanna C. Watson and Leslie S. Greenberg, "Empathetic Resonance: A Neuroscience Perspective," in *The Social Neuroscience of Empathy*, eds. Jean Decety and William Ickes (Cambridge, MA: MIT Press, 2009), p. 126. See also Katherine P. Rankin et al., "Structural Anatomy of Empathy in Neurodegenerative Disease," *Brain* 129, no. 11 (2006), 2945–47 (summarizing research study to determine the degree to which regional differences in the brain volumes correspond to real-life empathic behavior).

51. Marco Iacoboni, "Understanding Others: Imitation, Language and Empathy," in *Perspectives on Imitation*, Hurley and Chater, pp. 77–101.

52. Susan Hurley and Nick Chater, eds., *Perspectives on Imitation: From Neuroscience to Social Science* 3 (Cambridge, MA: MIT Press, 2005).

53. Argye E. Hillis, "Inability to Empathize: Brain Lesions That Disrupt Sharing and Understanding Another's Emotions," *Brain* 137, no. 4 (2014), 983–4, 986.

54. Marco Iacoboni, *Mirroring People: The New Science of How We Connect with Others* (New York: Picador, 2008).

55. Watson and Greenberg, *Empathetic Resonance*, p. 127.

56. Elizabeth A. Reynolds Losin, et al., "Race Modulates Neural Activity During Imitation," *Neuroimage* 59, no. 4 (2012), 3594–5.

57. Watson and Greenberg, *Empathetic Resonance*, p. 126.

58. For a survey of this research, see Elaine Hatfield, John T. Cacioppo, and Richard L. Rapson, *Emotional Contagion* (Cambridge: Cambridge University Press, 1994), pp. 1–7 (discussing emotional contagion and its effects on social and developmental psychology).

59. See, for example, Paula M. Neidenthal, "Embodying Emotion," *Science* (May 18, 2007), 1104 (explaining a study that examined the brain activity of a participant watching another participant experience pain in an attempt to prove that an individual can feel another's emotions).

60. Jamil Zaki et al., "The Neural Bases of Empathic Accuracy," *PNAS* 106, no. 27 (2009), 11384.

61. Ullrich Wagner et al., "The Relationship Between Trait Empathy and Memory Formation for Social vs. Non-Social Information," *BMC Psychology* 3, no. 2 (2015), 1 (clarifying the distinction between cognitive empathy where one mentally represents another's thoughts, and affective empathy where one aligns with another's emotional state); Clifford B. Saper, "The Central Autonomic Nervous System: Conscious Visceral Perception and Autonomic Pattern Generation," *Annual Review of Neuroscience* 25 (2002), 453–61 (describing patterns of autonomic responses in the central nervous system); Kevin A. Keay and Richard Bandler , "Parallel Circuits Mediating Distinct Emotional Coping Reactions to Different Types of Stress," *Neuroscience & Biobehavioral Reviews*, 25, no. 7–8 (2001), 669 (establishing that emotional coping strategies to different types of stress

arise through distinct, longitudinal neuronal columns of the midbrain periaqueductal gray (PAG) region).

62. Joel S. Milner, Lea B. Halsey, and Jim Fultz, "Empathic Responsiveness and Affective Reactivity to Infant Stimuli in High- and Low-Risk for Physical Child Abuse Mothers," *Child Abuse & Neglect* 19, no. 6 (1995), 767–8, 77 6.

63. Kahni Clements et al., "Empathic Accuracy of Intimate Partners in Violent Versus Nonviolent Relationships," *Personal Relationships* 14, no. 3 (2007), 370–1.

64. Christopher K. Hsee, E. Hatfield, and C. Chemtob, "Assessments of the Emotional States of Others: Conscious Judgments Versus Emotional Contagion," *Journal of Social and Clinical Psychology* 11 (1992), 119–21.

65. Samuel M. McClure et al., "Conflict Monitoring Cognition-Emotion Competition," in *Handbook of Emotion Regulation*, 1st ed., ed. James J. Gross (New York: Guilford Press, 2007), 204, 205.

66. Wagner et al., "The Relationship Between Trait Empathy and Memory Formation," 7. Jean Decety and Philip L. Jackson, "The Functional Architecture of Human Empathy," *Behavioral & Cognitive Neuroscience Reviews* 3, no. 2 (2004), 73–5 (proposing empathy as an "innate ability to recognize that the self and the other can be the same").

67. See, generally, Gross, *Handbook of Emotion Regulation*. See McClure et al., "Conflict Monitoring Cognition-Emotion Competition," 222 (concluding that there are at least three types of decision making where emotions discernibly influence behavior).

68. Vartanian and Mandel, *The Neuroscience of Decision Making*; Bechara, *Human Emotions in Decision Making*, 73. See Jan De Houwer and Dick Hermans, "Do Feelings Have a Mind of Their Own?" in *Cognition & Emotion: Reviews of Current Research and Theories* 28 (2010).

69. Bechara, *Human Emotions in Decision Making*, 74: "Neurobiological studies about emotion are complex and have lagged behind other studies of mind and brain but support exists for the idea that decision making is a process critically dependent on neural systems important for the processing of emotions, conscious knowledge alone is not sufficient for making advantageous decisions, and ... emotion is not always beneficial to decision making[;] [s]ometimes it can be disruptive."

70. For early ground-breaking work in this area, see António Damásio, *Descartes' Error: Emotion, Reason and the Human Brain* (New York: Penguin Books, 1994) (demonstrating that emotions play a significant role in social cognition and in decision making). For more recent work, see António Damásio and G.B. Carvalho, "The Nature of Feelings: Evolutionary and Neurobiological Origins," *Nature Reviews Neuroscience* 14, no. 2 (2013), 143–52.

71. Bechara, *Human Emotions in Decision Making*, 75–7.
72. Antoine Bechara and Nasir Naqvi, "The Somatovisceral Components of Emotions and Their Role in Decision Making: Specific Attention to the Ventromedial Prefrontal Cortex," in *Handbook of Neuroscience for the Behavioral Sciences*, eds. Gary G. Berntson and John T. Cacioppo (Hoboken, NJ: Wiley, 2009), pp. 1, 751 ("The choices they make are no longer advantageous—the patients often decide against their best interests—and are remarkably different from the kinds of choices they were known to make in the pre-morbid period. They are unable to learn from previous mistakes").
73. Bechara and Naqvi, "The Somatovisceral Components of Emotions" ("As noted, the patients have normal intellect, as measured by a variety of conventional neuropsychological tests").
74. Vartanian and Mandel, *The Neuroscience of Decision Making*, 76 ("Deprived of these emotional signals, patients must rely on a slow cost-benefit analysis of various conflicting options").
75. See E.T. Rolls, *The Brain and Emotion* (Oxford: Oxford University Press, 1999). Tiago V. Maia and James L. McClelland, "A Reexamination of the Evidence for the Somatic Marker Hypothesis: What Participants Really Know in the Iowa Gambling Task," *PNAS* 101, no. 45 (2004), 16075–80.
76. António R. Damásio, "The Somatic Marker Hypothesis and the Possible Functions of the Prefrontal Cortex," *Philosophical Transactions: Biological Sciences* 351, no. 1346 (1996), 1413–20.
77. Antoine Bechara, Hanna Damasio, and António R. Damásio, "Emotion, Decision Making and the Orbitofrontal Cortex," *Cerebral Cortex* 10, no. 3 (2000), 295–307 ("The somatic marker hypothesis proposes that a defect in emotion and feeling plays an important role in impaired decision making"). Vartanian and Mandel, 86: "[T]he results provide strong support for the notion that decision-making is guided by emotional signaling (or somatic states) generated in anticipation of future events. Without the ability to generate these emotional/somatic signals, the patients fail to avoid the [choices] that lead to painful losses."
78. Antoine Bechara, Hanna Damasio, and António R. Damásio, "Emotion, Decision Making and the Orbitofrontal Cortex," 10 *Cerebral Cortex*, issue 3, (March 2000), 295–307.
79. Antoine Bechara, "Human Emotions in Decision Making: Are They Useful or Disruptive?" in Vartanian and Mandel, eds., *The Neuroscience of Decision Making*, pp. 73–95.
80. Bechara, "Human Emotions in Decision Making," pp. 87–9 (explaining that the VM cortex "couples knowledge to representations of 'what it feels like' to be in certain situations").

81. Bechara, p. 88 (explaining how the VM prefrontal cortex couples information to emotional representations, with one function serving as a "trigger structure for somatic/emotional states from secondary inducers").

82. Bechara, p. 85 ("The function of the amygdala is to couple the features of the object with its emotional attribute. For example, a snake is simply an object with certain features. However, this object is linked to some emotional attribute such as fear").

83. Bechara, p. 86 (explaining that the amygdala embraces the "fight or flight" response).

84. George F. Loewenstein et al., "Risk as Feelings" *Psychological Bulletin* 127, no. 2 (2001), 267.

85. For early groundbreaking work in this area, see Damasio, *Descartes' Error* (demonstrating that emotions play a significant role in social cognition and in decision making). For more recent work on the topic, see Damasio Carvalho, "The Nature of Feelings," 143 (examining the evolutionary and neurobiological origins of feelings).

86. For emergent scholarship taking such an approach, see Bradley, "Cognitive Competence in Executive Branch Decision Making"; Paul S. Davies and Peter A. Alces, "Neuroscience Changes More Than You Can Think," *Journal of Law, Technology & Policy* 2017, no. 1 (2017). For work on neuroscience, law, and decision making, see, for example, M. Freeman, ed., *Law and Neuroscience: Current Legal Issues*, vol. 13 (Oxford: Oxford University Press, 2011); Oliver R. Goodenough, "Mapping Cortical Areas Associated with Legal Reasoning and Moral Intuition" *Jurimetrics* 41, no. 4 (2001), 431 (discussing how to conceptualize law in response to insights from neuroscience).

87. Bechara, "Human Emotions in Decision Making," 76.

88. Bechara, 76.

89. Bechara, 76–7.

90. There are many studies exploring the relationship between emotion and decision making. See, for example, Baba Shiv, George Lowenstein, and Antonie Bechara, "The Dark Side of Emotion in Decision-Making: When Individuals With Decreased Emotional Reactions Make More Advantageous Decisions," *Cognitive Brain Research* 23, no. 1 (2005), 85–92; www.ncbi.nlm.nih.gov/pubmed/15795136.

91. See Kitty Xu et al., "Neural Basis of Cognitive Control over Movement Inhibition: Human fMRI and Primate Electrophysiology Evidence," *Neuron* 96, no. 6 (2017). See generally Bret Stetka, "The Neuroscience of Changing Your Mind," *Scientific American*, December 7, 2017, https://perma.cc/4PYM-BCVQ.

92. Peter Graf and Michael E.J. Masson, eds., *Implicit Memory: New Directions in Cognition, Development and Neuropsychology* (Mahwah,

NJ: Lawrence Erlbaum Associates, 1993). See also Patricia Churchland, Touching a Nerve: The Self as Brain (New York: W.W. Norton and Company, 2013), pp. 197–8 (describing the concept of "hidden cognition" from a psychological perspective and discussing the distinctions between conscious, unconscious, subconscious and nonconscious); Rian E. McMullin, *The New Handbook of Cognitive Therapy Techniques* (New York: W.W. Norton and Company, 2000), p. 68: "The third cognition between emotion and behavior is a belief I call the hidden cognition. It is hidden because most clients are not aware of its existence. The [hidden belief] occurs after clients feel an emotion, but immediately before they engage in a behavior. Most clients don't notice this cognition because it is so rapid They experience it as a vague impression, an undigested conception often occurring before they can put it into words."

93. Joo-Hyun Song and Ken Nakayama, "Hidden Cognitive States Revealed in Choice Reaching Tasks," 13 *Trends in Cognitive Science* 13, no. 8 (2009), 360 ("Recent studies measuring continuous hand movements during target choice reaching tasks reveal the temporal evolution of hidden internal events").

94. See, generally, Ariely, *Predictably Irrational*.

95. For a review of recent studies, see Jennifer T. Kubota, Mahzarin R. Banaji, and Elizabeth A. Phelps, "The Neuroscience of Race," *Nature Neuroscience* 15, no. 7 (2012). See, generally, Joshua Gowin, "The Neuroscience of Racial Bias," *Psychology Today*, Aug. 20, 2012, www.psychologytoday.com/us/blog/ you-illuminated/201208/the-neuroscience-racial-bias [https://perma.cc/H267 -9VH5]; Chris Bergonzi, "Understanding Bias and the Brain," Korn Ferry Institute, *Briefings Magazine*, May 11, 2015; www.kornferry.com/institute/un derstanding-bias-and-brain [https://perma.cc/AQ3V-TE3E].

96. Joseph LeDoux, "The Amygdala," *Current Biology* 17, no. 20 (2007).

97. Adam M. Chekroud, Jim A.C. Everett, Holly Bridge, and Miles Hewstone, "A Review of Neuroimaging Studies of Race-Related Prejudice: Does Amygdala Response Reflect Threat?" *Front Hum. Neurosci.* 8, no. 179 (2014); www.ncbi.nlm.nih.gov/pmc/articles/PMC3973920/. "We suggest that differential amygdala activity may best be considered in terms of threat, and we correspondingly highlight studies demonstrating bilateral amygdala modulation by threat. More specifically, we then argue that negative culturally-learned associations between black males and potential threat may better explain the data than does a general ingroup–outgroup explanation."

98. Jennifer Kubota, Mahzarin R. Banaji, and Elizabeth A. Phelps, "The Neuroscience of Race, *Nature Neuroscience* 15, no. 7 (2012), 940–8, https://dash.harvard.edu/handle/1/33471144.

4 HUMAN CHOICE AT THE INTERNATIONAL COURT OF JUSTICE

1. Benjamin N. Cardozo, *The Nature of the Judicial Process* (New Haven, CT: Yale University Press, 1921), p. 12.
2. The ICJ is the principal judicial organ of the United Nations. UN Charter, Art. 7 (1945), www.un.org/en/sections/un-charter/introductory-note/index .html.
3. See Karen J. Alter, *The New Terrain of International Law: Courts, Politics, Rights* (Princeton, NJ: Princeton University Press, 2014), pp. 10–16 (sharing her views that international courts have four different roles consisting of dispute settlement, administrative review, enforcement, and constitutional review).
4. Statute of the International Court of Justice, Art. 10(3) ICJ judges are first nominated by eligible national groups from the Permanent Court of Arbitration. The UN secretary-general then prepares a list of those nominated who are also eligible to serve on the court. Both the UN General Assembly and the UN Security Council then vote, separately, taking into account both the individual and the collective representation on the ICJ. People who receive a majority vote in both the General Assembly and the Security Council are elected. The exception to this occurs in the event that two people of the same nationality are elected and, in that case, the older of them shall serve. Judges serve for nine-year terms and are eligible for reelection. When the ICJ Statute was being negotiated, states agreed that judges should be independent and should operate as such regardless of the nation that they came from. The only additional formal requirements that the ICJ Statute specifies is that judges possess high moral character and the standard of qualification necessary in their own country to serve in the highest judicial office. Statute of the International Court of Justice, Art. 2
5. Alter, *The New Terrain of International Law*, pp. 8–9 (discussing different views of the power that international judges have).
6. "If any party to a case fails to perform the obligations incumbent upon it under a judgment rendered by the Court, the other party may have recourse to the Security Council, which may, if it deems necessary, make recommendations or decide upon measures to be taken to give effect to the judgment." UN Charter, Art. 92.2 (1945) www.un.org/en/sections/un-charter/chapter-xiv/index.html.
7. A. Mark Weisburd, *Failings of the International Court of Justice* (Oxford: Oxford University Press, 2016); Robert Kolb, *The International Court of Justice* (Portland, OR: Hart Publishing, 2013); Ruth Mackenzie, Cesare P. R. Romano, Yuval Shany, and Phillipe Sands, *Manual on International Courts and Tribunals* (Oxford: Oxford University Press, 2010); John Collier

and Vaughan Lowe, *The Settlement of Disputes in International Law* (Oxford: Oxford University Press, 1999); Higgins, *Problems and Processes*.

8. Philippa Webb, *International Judicial Integration and Fragmentation* (Oxford: Oxford University Press, 2013).

9. Alter, *The New Terrain of International Law*, p. 32 ("International courts have the power to issue binding rulings in cases that are adjudicated").

10. Alter, *The New Terrain of International Law*, p. 19 ("International relations scholarship generally conceives of international courts as a cipher of state interests").

11. Deeper inquiries into the biographies of those who have served on the court are less common. See Ruth Mackenzie et al., eds., *Selecting International Judges: Principle, Process, and Politics* (Oxford: Oxford University Press, 2010); Daniel Terris, Cesare P.R. Romano, and Leigh Swigart, *The International Judge: An Introduction to the Men and Women Who Decide the World's Cases* (Lebanon, NH: Brandeis University Press, 2007). There is, of course, a rich literature on judicial behavior in domestic courts, which enjoy a certain relevance to the study of judges in international law. See, for example, Robert M. Howard and Kirk A. Randazzo, eds., *Routledge Handbook of Judicial Behavior*, (New York: Routledge, 2018); Benjamin Alarie and Andrew J. Green, *Commitment and Cooperation on High Courts, A Cross-Country Examination of Institutional Constraints on Judges* (Oxford: Oxford University Press, 2017); Jeremy Cooper, ed., *Being a Judge in the Modern World* (Oxford: Oxford University Press, 2017) (providing analysis from judges and scholars); Nuno Garoupa and Tom Ginsburg, *Judicial Reputation* (Chicago, IL: Chicago University Press, 2015); Lawrence Baum, *The Puzzle of Judicial Behavior* (Ann Arbor, MI: University of Michigan Press, 2004) (exploring judicial goals and their impact on judicial decisions).

12. The research on judicial behavior is too vast to cite here. For a good reference point, see Richard A. Posner, *How Judges Think* (Cambridge, MA: Harvard University Press, 2008) (describing nine theories of judicial behavior and exploring judicial emotion and intuition in the context of the US Supreme Court); Lee Epstein, William M. Landes, and Richard Posner, *Behavior of Federal Judges: A Theoretical and Empirical Study of Rational Choice* (Cambridge, MA: Harvard University Press, 2013).

13. Lucy Reed, "Observations on the Relationship between Diplomatic and Judicial Means of Dispute Settlement," in *Diplomatic and Judicial Means of Dispute Settlement*, eds. Laurence Boisson de Chazournes, Marcelo G. Kohen, and Jorge E. Viñuales (Boston, MA: Martinus Nijhoff Publishers, 2013), p. 291 ("[W]hat impact does diplomatic training have on judicial decision-makers?").

14. Alter, *The New Terrain of International Law*.

15. Mark Drumbl, "The Expressive Value of Prosecuting and Punishing Terrorists: Hamdan, the Geneva Conventions and International Criminal Law," *George Washington Law Review* 75, no. 5/6 (2007). Garoupa and Ginsburg, *Judicial Reputation*; Eric A. Posner, "Does Political Bias in the Judiciary Matter? Implications of Judicial Bias Studies for Legal and Constitutional Reform," *University of Chicago Law Review* 75, no. 2 (2008); Baum, *The Puzzle of Judicial Behavior* (exploring judicial goals and their impact on judicial decisions).

16. "Documenting Numbers of Victims of the Holocaust and Nazi Persecution," United States Holocaust Memorial Museum, last modified February 4, 2019, www.ushmm.org/wlc/en/article.php?Module Id=10008193 (estimates are based on Nazi reports and postwar demographic studies).

17. "Cambodian Genocide Program," Yale University Genocide Studies Program, accessed January 11, 2020, http://gsp.yale.edu/case-studies/cam bodian-genocide-program (estimating 1.7 million or 21 percent of the national population).

18. "Rwanda Project," Yale University Genocide Studies Program, accessed January 11, 2020, http://gsp.yale.edu/case-studies/rwanda-project (estimating up to 90 percent of pre-1994 Tutsi population were murdered).

19. Convention on the Prevention and Punishment of the Crime of Genocide, Dec. 9, 1948, 78 UNTS 277. At present, 147 nations have either signed or acceded the Genocide Convention. See "Treaties, States Parties and Commentaries," International Committee of the Red Cross, accessed January 11, 2020, https://ihl-databases.icrc.org/applic/ihl/ihl.nsf/States.xsp? xp_viewStates=XPages_NORMStatesParties&xp_treatySelected=357.

20. The Rome Statute (entered into force 2002, adopted 1998) www.icc-cpi.int /resource-library/documents/rs-eng.pdf; Application of the Convention on the Prevention and Punishment of the Crime of Genocide (*Bosnia and Herzegovina* v. *Serbia and Montenegro*), Judgment, ICJ Reports 2007, pp. 425–50 (affirming states' obligation to prevent and punish the crime of genocide).

21. Convention on the Prevention and Punishment of the Crime of Genocide, Art. 2, defines the crime thus: "In the present Convention, genocide means any of the following acts committed with intent to destroy, in whole or in part, a national, ethnical, racial or religious group, as such: (a) Killing members of the group; (b) Causing serious bodily or mental harm to members of the group; (c) Deliberately inflicting on the group conditions of life calculated to bring about its physical destruction in whole or in part; (d) Imposing measures intended to prevent births within the group; (e) Forcibly transferring children of the group to another group."

22. Claims of alleged genocide have been heard at the ICJ, International Criminal Court, International Criminal Tribunal for the former Yugoslavia, International Criminal Tribunal for Rwanda, European Court of Human Rights, Inter-American Court of Human Rights, Iraqi Special Tribunal, and the Extraordinary Chambers in the Courts of Cambodia. Webb, *International Judicial Integration and Fragmentation*, p. 14.

23. Statute of the International Court of Justice, Art. 20.

24. Reservations to the Convention on the Prevention and Punishment of the Crime of Genocide (Advisory Opinion) 1951 ICJ Rep 23.

25. For case background and proceedings see "Armed Activities on the Territory of the Congo (New Application: 2002) (*Democratic Republic of the Congo v. Rwanda*) Overview of the Case," International Court of Justice, www.icj-cij.org/files/case-related/126/126-20060203-JUD-01-00-EN.pdf.

26. *Case Concerning Armed Activities on the Territory of the Congo (Dem. Rep. of the Congo v. Rwanda), Judgment, 2005 ICJ*, para. 39. ("The Court also notes that the Parties take opposing views, first on whether, in adopting *décret-loi* No. 014/01 of 15 February 1995, Rwanda effectively withdrew its reservation to Article IX of the Genocide Convention and, secondly, on the question of the legal effect of the statement by Rwanda's Minister of Justice at the Sixty-first Session of the United Nations Commission on Human Rights.")

27. *Case Concerning Armed Activities.*

28. Reservations to the Convention on the Prevention and Punishment of the Crime of Genocide (Advisory Opinion) 1951 ICJ Rep 15, 23.

29. Armed Activities on the Territory of the Congo (New Application: 2002) (*Democratic Republic of the Congo v. Rwanda*), Jurisdiction and Admissibility, Judgment, ICJ Reports 2006, p. 6.

30. *DRC v. Rwanda*, Judgment para. 125: "Finally, the Court deems it necessary to recall that the mere fact that rights and obligations *erga omnes* or peremptory norms of general inter- national law *(jus cogens)* are at issue in a dispute cannot in itself constitute an exception to the principle that its jurisdiction always depends on the consent of the parties (see paragraph 64 above)."

31. *Case Concerning Armed Activities*, para. 59: "The DRC argues finally that, even if the Court were to reject its argument based on the peremptory character of the norms contained in the Genocide Convention, it cannot permit Rwanda to behave in a contradictory fashion, that is to say, to call on the United Nations Security Council to set up an international criminal tribunal to try the authors of the genocide committed against the Rwandan people, while at the same time refusing to allow those guilty of genocide to be tried when they are Rwandan nationals or the victims of the genocide are not Rwandans."

32. The Court also addressed *jus cogens* in Jurisdictional Immunities of the State, 2012 ICJ Rep 99. For further analysis see, for example,

Hugh Thirlway, *The International Court of Justice* (Oxford: Oxford University Press, 2016), p. 31: "The concept, therefore, while widely recognized, still lacks, to this extent, judicial confirmation: nor is there complete unanimity among scholars or among States that the concept has a real existence, in the form generally asserted, in general customary law."; Weisburd, *Failings of the International Court of Justice*, p. 78 ("the concept of *jus cogens* make no sense").

33. Consisting of the fifteen elected judges and the two ad hoc judges.

34. *Case Concerning Armed Activities on the Territory of the Congo (Dem. Rep. of the Congo v. Rwanda), Judgment* (Separate Opinion of judges Higgins, Kooijmans, Elaraby, Owada and Simma) 2006 ICJ Rep. 6, para. 25.

35. Interview with Bruno Simma, Judge Iran-US Claims Tribunal, former judge, International Court of Justice (2003–2012), Professor of Law, University of Michigan School of Law.

36. *Case Concerning Armed Activities on the Territory of the Congo (Dem. Rep. of the Congo v. Rwanda), Judgment* (Declaration by Judge Elaraby) 2006 ICJ Rep. 6, para. 1.

37. *Case Concerning Armed Activities on the Territory of the Congo (Dem. Rep. of the Congo v. Rwanda), Judgment* (Dissenting Opinion of Judge Koroma), [2006] ICJ Rep 6, para. 24.

38. Interview with Bruno Simma.

39. Interview with Thomas Buergenthal, Lobingier Professor Emeritus of Comparative Law and Jurisprudence, George Washington University School of Law, former judge, International Court of Justice (2000–2010), former president and judge, Inter-American Court of Human Rights (1979–1991) (January 15, 2017).

40. Interview with Bruno Simma.

41. Interview with Thomas Buergenthal.

42. Interview with Thomas Buergenthal.

43. Interview with Bruno Simma.

44. Interview with Thomas Buergenthal.

45. Interview with Georges Abi-Saab, Honorary Professor of International Law at the Graduate Institute of International and Development Studies, former judge ad hoc, International Court of Justice (October 13, 2016).

46. Interview with Bruno Simma.

47. *Case Concerning the Vienna Convention on Consular Relations (Paraguay v. U.S.), Request for the Indication of Provisional Measures, Order of April 9*, 1998 ICJ Rep 248.

48. *Case Concerning the Vienna Convention on Consular Relations (Paraguay v. U.S.), Request for the Indication of Provisional Measures, Order of April 9* (Declaration of Judge Oda), 1998 ICJ Rep 262, para. 8.

49. *LaGrand Case (Germany v. U.S.), Judgement*, 2001 ICJ Rep 525.

50. *LaGrand Case (Germany v. U.S.), Order on the Request for Indication of Provisional Measures, March 3, 1999*, ICJ Reports 1999, p. 9.
51. *LaGrand Case (Germany v. U.S.), Order on the Request for Indication of Provisional Measures, March 3, 1999* (Declaration of Judge Oda), para.7.
52. *LaGrand Case (Germany v. U.S.)* (Dissenting Opinion of Judge Oda) 2001 ICJ Rep 525, 531, para. 15.
53. Thirlway, *The International Court of Justice*, p. 30. Hugh Thirlway asks "to what extent, if any, may humanitarian considerations of this kind impede the strict application of the law?"
54. Jeanne Gaakeer, *Judging From Experience: Law, Praxis, Humanities* (Edinburgh: Edinburgh University Press, 2019) (discussing judging from a civil law perspective and offering a "humanistic model for doing law"). Quote from p. 6.
55. See, generally, Gross, *Handbook of Emotion Regulation*.
56. Alain Berthoz, *Emotion and Reason: The Cognitive Neuroscience of Decision Making* (Oxford: Oxford University Press, 2006).
57. Vartanian and Mandel, *The Neuroscience of Decision Making*; Bechara, "Human Emotions in Decision Making," 73.
58. For the entire case docket in *The Prosecutor v. Duško Tadic*, see www.icty.org /en/case/tadic. Rosa Aloisi and James Meernik, *Judgment Day: Judicial Decision Making at the International Criminal Tribunals* (Cambridge: Cambridge University Press, 2017), pp. 113–14. (Discussing judicial expressivism, which the authors define as "the use of words to convey a moral judgment rather than serve a legal purpose" at the ICTY and noting that "[s]atements like those pronounced by Judge Robinson in the *Lukic* case stand out in international justice. Words of vivid condemnation and stigmatization of criminals have emerged as a potent expression of moral indignation.")
59. Interview with Georges Abi-Saab.
60. Interview with Georges Abi-Saab.
61. Erik Voeten, "The Impartiality of International Judges: Evidence from the European Court of Human Rights," *American Political Science Review* 102, no. 4 (2008), 417–33, https://ssrn.com/abstract=705363; Holger Spamann and Lars Klöhn, "Justice is Less Blind, and Less Legalistic, Than we Thought: Evidence from an Experiment with Real Judges," *Journal of Legal Studies* 45, no. 2 (2016), www.journals.uchicago.edu/doi/abs/10.1086/688861.
62. "Press Release 2004/28: Legal Consequences of the Construction of a Wall in the Occupied Palestinian Territory (Advisory Opinion)," International Court of Justice, July 9, 2004, www.icj-cij.org/files/case-related/131/131-20040709-PRE-01-00-EN.pdf.
63. Interview with Judge Buergenthal.
64. *Legal Consequences of the Construction of a Wall in the Occupied Palestinian Territory, Advisory Opinion* (Dissenting Opinion of Judge

Buergenthal), 2004 ICJ Rep 240, p. 9, para. 10: "At the same time, Article 17, paragraph 2, reflects much broader conceptions of justice and fairness that must be observed by courts of law than this Court appears to acknowledge. Judicial ethics are not matters strictly of hard and fast rules – I doubt that they can ever be exhaustively defined – they are matters of perception and of sensibility to appearances that courts must continuously keep in mind to preserve their legitimacy."

65. Buergenthal (Dissenting Opinion) p. 8 providing a partial quote of Elaraby's interview: "Today, he [Judge Elaraby] is concerned about a tendency to play into Israel's hands, and thus to marginalise the crux of the Arab Israeli conflict, which is the illegitimate occupation of territory. 'It has long been very clear that Israel, to gain time, has consistently followed the policy known as "establishing new facts". This time factor, with respect to any country, is a tactical element [in negotiations], but for the Israelis it is a strategy.' New facts and new problems are created on the ground in this manner, he explains, and the older, essential problems are forgotten. Grave violations of humanitarian law ensue: the atrocities perpetrated on Palestinian civilian populations, for instance, but also such acts as the recent occupation of the PNA's headquarters. 'I hate to say it', Elaraby continues, 'but you do not see the Palestinians, or any other Arab country today, presenting the issue thus when addressing the international community: Israel is occupying Palestinian territory, and the occupation itself is against international law. Israel has twice, in writing, with the whole world as witness, committed itself to the implementation of UN Security Council resolution 242 on the occupied territories: once at Camp David with Egypt [in 1978], and once in Oslo with the Palestinians [in 1993].' Very recently, he adds, the Sharon government launched a new strategy, wreaking confusion and gaining time by describing territories Israel has already recognised as occupied as 'disputed'. All these, explains Elaraby, 'are attempts to confuse the issues and complicate any serious attempt to get Israel out of the occupied territories. You can negotiate security, which will be mutual for both parties, but you cannot negotiate whether to leave or not.'"

66. "Press Release 2004/4: Legal Consequences of the Construction of a Wall in the Occupied Palestinian Territory," International Court of Justice, February 3, 2004, www.icj-cij.org/files/case-related/131/131-20040203-PRE -01-00-EN.pdf.

67. "Press Release 2004/4," para. 10.

68. Interview with Bruno Simma.

69. Interview with Bruno Simma.

70. Interview with Bruno Simma.

71. Interview with George Abi-Saab.

72. Interview with Laurence Boisson de Chazournes, international arbitrator and Professor of International Law, University of Geneva, July 22, 2020.

73. Interview with Joan Donoghue Judge, International Court of Justice (elected President of the ICJ on February 8, 2021) (2010–present) (July 25, 2018).
74. Anonymous, interview on file with author.
75. Interview with Lucy F. Reed, arbitrator, professor and director, Centre for International Law, National University of Singapore, vice president, ICC Court of Arbitration (July 10, 2018).
76. Paul Zak, *Trust Factor: The Science of Creating High-Performance Companies* (New York: AMACOM, 2017), p. 16.
77. Michael Kosfeld, "Trust in the Brain: Neurobiological Determinants of Human Social Behavior," *EMBO Reports* 8, no. S1 (2007); Jan Born et al., "Sniffing Neuropeptides: A Transnasal Approach to the Human Brain," *Nature Neuroscience* 5, no. 6; Michael Kosfeld et al., "Oxytocin Increases Trust in Humans."
78. See, for example, Terris, Romano and Swigart, *The International Judge*, 49 (International judges' "primary task is to consider the facts and substantive points of the cases before them in accordance with the law").
79. Eve Gerber, "Stephen Breyer on His Intellectual Influences," Five Books, accessed January 11, 2020, https://fivebooks.com/best-books/stephen-breyer-intellectual-influences/.
80. Posner, *How Judges Think*, p. 107: "Unconscious preconceptions, which play so large a role in the judicial process and are the key to reconciling the attitudinal literature with what judges think they are doing, are products of intuition."
81. Spain Bradley, "Advancing Neuroscience in International Law."
82. Doron Teichman and Eyal Zamir, "Judicial Decision-Making: A Behavioral Perspective" in *The Oxford Handbook of Behavioral Economics and the Law*, eds. Eyal Zamir and Doron Teichman (Oxford: Oxford University Press, 2014); *The Psychology of Judicial Decision Making* (David Klein and Gregory Mitchell, eds., 2008). For empirical approaches to studying judicial and arbitrator behavior (some of which also employ a behavioral approach), see, generally, Linda A. Berger, "A Revised View of the Judicial Hunch," 10 *Legal Communication and Rhetoric* issue 1, 17–18 (2013); Susan Franck et al., "Inside the Arbitrator's Mind," 66 *Emory Law Journal* 1115 (2017); Chris Guthrie et al., "Blinking on the Bench: How Judges Decide Cases," 93 *Cornell Law Review* issue 1 (2007); Chris Guthrie, Jeffrey J. Rachlinski, and Andrew J. Wistrich, "Inside the Judicial Mind," 86 *Cornell Law Review* 777 (2001).
83. Empirical studies on US Supreme Court judges, for example, have studied how factors such as college education, choice of law school, geographic location when they were young, age, gender, racial, and national identities influence their decisions have identified these explanatory variables with differing correlations. See C. Neal Tate and

Roger Handberg , "Time Binding and Theory Building in Personal Attribute Models of Supreme Court Voting Behavior, 1916–88," *American Journal of Political Science* 35, no. 2 (1991); Orley Ashenfelter, Theodore Eisenberg, and Stewart Schwab, "Politics and the Judiciary: The Influence of Judicial Background on Case Outcomes," *Journal of Legal Studies* 24, no. 2 (1995).

84. "Report of the International Court of Justice 1 August 2005–31 July 2006," International Court of Justice, August 14, 2006, Supplement No. 4 (A/61/4), 2, para. 11, www.icj-cij.org/files/annual-reports/2005-2006-en.pdf.

85. "Report of the International Court of Justice," 2, para. 10.

86. The case was the first of its kind where allegations of genocide had been made by one state against another. The court determined that Serbia had violated its obligation to prevent the Srebrenica genocide per Article 1 of the Genocide Convention. The court did not characterize alleged atrocities and killings throughout Bosnia and Herzegovina as genocide due to the lack of their finding of specific intent.

5 HUMAN CHOICE AT THE UN SECURITY COUNCIL

1. John Danforth, US Ambassador to the United Nations (July 1, 2004–January 20, 2005). Quote found in Linda Fasulo, *An Insider's Guide to the UN*, 3rd ed. (New Haven, CT: Yale University Press, 2015), p. 54.

2. Carol Morello, "U.N. Security Council Members Divided on Military Action in Syria," Washington Post (Oct. 10, 2019) www.washingtonpost.com/nation al-security/un-security-council-fails-to-condemn-turkeys-military-action-in-syria/2019/10/10/9bff99d0-eb87-11e9-9306-47cb0324fd44_story.html.

3. For background, see Lara Seligman, "Greenlighted by Trump, Turkey Invades Syria," *Foreign Policy* (Dec. 21, 2019) https://foreignpolicy.com/20 19/12/21/turkey-syria-kurds-invasion-trump/.

4. Carol Morello, "U.N. Security Council Members Divided on Turkey's Military Action in Syria," *Washington Post*, Oct. 10, 2019, www.washington post.com/national-security/un-security-council-fails-to-condemn-turkeys-military-action-in-syria/2019/10/10/9bff99d0-eb87-11e9-9306-47cb0324fd44_story.html.

5. UN Charter, Art. 2(4): "All members shall refrain in their international relations from the threat or use of force against the territorial integrity or political independence of any state, or in any other manner inconsistent with the purposes of the United Nations."

6. UN Charter, chapter 7.

7. UN Charter, Art. 51: "Nothing in the present Charter shall impair the inherent right of individual or collective self-defence if an armed attack occurs against a Member of the United Nations, until the Security Council has taken measures necessary to maintain international peace and security.

Measures taken by Members in the exercise of this right of self-defence shall be immediately reported to the Security Council and shall not in any way affect the authority and responsibility of the Security Council under the present Charter to take at any time such action as it deems necessary in order to maintain or restore international peace and security."

8. Jack Goldsmith and Eric Posner, *The Limits of International Law* (Oxford: Oxford University Press, 2005), pp. 167–84; Michael Glennon, *The Fog of Law: Pragmatism, Security and International Law* (Washington, DC: Wilson Center Press, 2010), pp. 44–50.

9. "States periodically conduct and, as a group, endorse operations that cannot plausibly be justified under them. What's significant is that, in these cases, states do not always try to hide their conduct or defend it by advancing controversial interpretations of the standards. Sometimes, they indicate that their positions rest on the facts of a case and are not meant to reflect or inform any general standard of law." Monica Hakimi, "The Jus ad Bellum's Regulatory Form," *American Journal of International Law* 112, no. 2 (2018), 153. Ian Johnstone, "Condoning the Use of Force: The UN Security Council as Interpreter of the Jus ad Bellum," *American Journal of International Law Unbound* 112 (2018).

10. As was argued by Holger Neimann, *The Justification of Responsibility in the UN Security Council: Practice of Normative Ordering in International Relations* (New York: Routledge, 2019); Michael C. Wood, "The Interpretation of Security Council Resolutions," in *Max Planck Yearbook of United Nations Law*, eds. Jochen A. Frowein and Rüdiger Wolfrum (London: Kluwer Law International, 1998), 2:78–9; Dapo Akande, "The International Court of Justice and the Security Council: Is there Room for Judicial Control of Decisions of the Political Organs of the United Nations?" *International and Comparative Law Quarterly*, 46, no. 2 (1997); Frederic L. Kirgis Jr., "The Security Council's First Fifty Years," *American Journal of International Law* 89, no. 3 (1995). Scholars also consider the unique powers of the Security Council and its quasi-judicial nature. Nigel D. White and Matthew Saul, "Legal Means of Dispute Settlement in the Field of Collective Security: The Quasi-Judicial Powers of the Security Council," in *International Law and Dispute Settlement: New Problems and Techniques*, eds. Duncan French, Matthew Saul, and Nigel D. White (Portland, OR: Hart Publishing, 2010), p. 193.

11. Ian Johnstone, "Legislation and Adjudication in the UN Security Council: Bringing Down the Deliberative Deficit," *American Journal of International Law* 102, no. 2 (2008).

12. Bruce Cronin and Ian Hurd, eds., *The UN Security Council and the Politics of International Authority* (London: Routledge, 2008); Ian Hurd, *After Anarchy: Legitimacy and Power in the United Nations Security Council* (Princeton, NJ: Princeton University Press, 2007), p. 84; H.

G. Nicholas, *The United Nations as a Political Institution*, 5th ed. (London: Oxford University Press, 1975).

13. Edward C. Luck, *UN Security Council: Practice and Promise* (London: Routledge, 2006); Vaughn Lowe, Jennifer Welsh, Dominik Zaum, eds., *The United Nations Security Council and War: The Evolution of Thought and Practice Since 1945* (Oxford: Oxford University Press, 2008).

14. David L. Bosco, *Five to Rule Them All: The UN Security Council and the Making of the Modern World* (Oxford: Oxford University Press, 2009). See, for example, Diana Panke, "Dwarfs in International Negotiations: How Small States Make Their Voices Heard." *Cambridge Review of International Affairs* 25, no. 3 (2012); Mary Whelan, "Ireland's Campaign for Election in 2000 to the United Nations Security Council," *Administration* 50, no. 1 (2002); Jeanne A.K. Hey, ed., *Small States in World Politics: Explaining Foreign Policy Behavior* (Boulder, CO: Lynne Rienner, 2003).

15. Neta C. Crawford, *Argument and Change in World Politics: Ethics, Decolonization and Humanitarian Intervention* (Cambridge: Cambridge University Press, 2002).

16. Ian Johnstone, *The Power of Deliberation: International Law, Politics, and Organizations* (Oxford: Oxford University Press, 2011), p. 14 (linking international relations literature of social constructivists to "deliberative democrats, who see the possibility of reasoned exchange beyond the level of the nation-state" and claiming that "legal argumentation an democratic deliberation are a measure of the legitimacy of decision making in IOs").

17. Bruce Cronin and Ian Hurd, "Introduction," in Cronin and Hurd, *The UN Security Council.*

18. Carmen Suro-Bredie, former assistant US trade representative for Latin America, the Caribbean, and Africa, https://ustr.gov/archive/Who_We_Are/Bios/Carmen_Suro-Bredie.html.

19. Jerald A. Combs, *American Diplomatic History: Two Centuries of Changing Interpretations* (Berkeley, CA: University of California Press, 1983), p. 158.

20. "Current Members," United Nations Security Council, www.un.org/securitycouncil/content/current-members.

21. UN Charter, Chapter V (1945).

22. See Michael J. Matheson, *Council Unbound: The Growth of UN Decision Making On Conflict And Postconflict Issues After The Cold War* (Washington, DC: United States Institute of Peace, 2006), pp. 33–7 ("[D]ecisions under Chapter VII take precedence over other sources of international law." The Council also has the authority to "require states to take actions that would otherwise be prohibited by other treaties."); Kirgis, "The Security Council's First Fifty Years" (the UNSC was "the best (in

fact, the only) judge of what amounts to a threat to international peace for purposes of chapter VII"); Rüdiger Wolfrum and Dieter Fleck, "Enforcement of International Humanitarian Law," in *The Handbook Of International Humanitarian Law*, 2nd ed., ed. Dieter Fleck (Oxford: Oxford University Press, 2008), p. 717: "Under Chapter VII of the UN Charter the Security Council is empowered to take far-reaching decisions ... In doing so, the Council enjoys considerable discretion."

23. International Commission on Intervention and State Sovereignty, The Responsibility To Protect ¶ 6.12 (2001). See also, UN General Assembly, Resolution 60/12005 World Summit Outcome, A/RES/60/1, ¶ 138 (September 16, 2005) (establishing widespread state support for the principle of R2P); UN Security Council, Resolution 1674, S/RES/1674, ¶ 4 (April 28, 2006); UN Secretary-General, Implementing the Responsibility to Protect, A/63/677, ¶¶ 8–9 (January 12, 2009).

24. UN Charter, Arts. 25, 48.

25. UN Charter, Art. 39, para. 1: "The Security Council shall determine the existence of any threat to the peace, breach of the peace, or act of aggression and shall make recommendations, or decide what measures shall be taken in accordance with Articles 41 and 42, to maintain or restore international peace and security."

26. US Department of State, "Postwar Foreign Policy Preparation, 1939–1945,"(1950) 576–81, reprinted in *A History of The United Nations Charter*, eds. Ruth B. Russell and Jeanette E. Muther (Washington, DC: Brookings Institution, 1958), p. 993.

27. UN Security Council, Resolution 660, S/RES/660, ¶¶ 1–4 (Aug. 2, 1990).

28. Wolfrum and Fleck, "Enforcement of International Humanitarian Law," 718 (noting, for example, that Chapter VII powers were traditionally invoked only in cases of a military breach of peace so the UNSC could undertake efforts to protect human rights and international humanitarian law only in this context).

29. UN Security Council, Provisional Rules of Procedure of the Security Council, S/96/Rev. 7 (Dec. 21, 1982). See also UN Charter, Arts. 24–6.

30. UN Charter, Art. 27, para. 2: "Decisions of the Security Council on procedural matters shall be made by an affirmative vote of nine members." UN Security Council, Provisional Rules of Procedure, Rule 40.

31. UN Charter, Art. 27(3). All substantive decisions of the council must be made with "the concurring votes of the permanent Members."

32. Matheson, *Council Unbound*, p. 30: "One striking aspect of all these delegations of decision-making authority is that the process by which decisions are made by these bodies varies considerably and in no instance conforms to the voting rules of Article 27 of the Charter." UN Charter, Art. 27, para. 3.

33. UN General Assembly, Resolution 267(III), The Problem of Voting in the Security Council, A/792, April 14, 1949, https://undocs.org/en/A/RES/267 (III).

34. UN General Assembly, Resolution 267(III), ¶3 "Recommends to the permanent members of the Security Council, in order to avoid impairment of the usefulness and prestige of the Council through excessive use of the veto: (a) To consult together wherever feasible upon important decision to be taken by the Security Council; . . . (c) If there is not unanimity, to exercise the veto only when they consider the question of vital importance, taking into account the interest of the United Nations as a whole, and to state upon what ground they consider this condition to be present."

35. Bardo Fassbender, *UN Security Council Reform and the Right of Veto: A Constitutional Perspective* (The Hague: Kluwer Law International, 1998), p. 165: "The right of veto emerged as the main feature of a new hierarchy in international relations which had developed in the course of the war and which the major power were determined to maintain." See, also, Statement by the Delegations of the Four Sponsoring Governments on Voting Procedure in the Security Council (San Francisco Declaration), June 7, 1945, para. I9, https://history.state.gov/historicaldocuments/frus1945v01/d273. ("In view of the primary responsibilities of the permanent members, they could not be expected, in the present condition of the world, to assume the obligation to act in so serious a matter as the maintenance of international peace and security in consequence of a decision in which they had not concurred.")

36. Fassbender, *UN Security Council Reform and the Right of Veto*, p. 168: "In view of the traditionally strong isolationist sentiments in the United States, which had prevented the country from joining the League of Nations only twenty-five years ago, the President [Roosevelt] was glad to be able to present the veto as a powerful means which would safeguard American interest in the new organization as well as the constitutional prerogatives of Congress in foreign and military affairs."

37. Certain states opposed the veto powers of the Council. Australia put forward a proposal, supported by many, that the veto power should be limited to cases where the council was taking enforcement action, and thus should not apply to Chapter VI decisions about dispute settlement. Egypt argued that a four out of five vote by the P5 in favor of Chapter VII actions should be required. At the San Francisco Conference, in response to these critiques, the P5 suggested that they would not participate in the UN if agreement was not reached on their proposed security provisions and the veto power. Fassbender, *UN Security Council Reform and the Right of Veto*, pp. 166–70.

38. Quote found in Fasulo, *An Insider's Guide to the UN*, p. 66 (quoting Richard Gowan).

39. Fasulo, 68 (quoting Colin Keating, former New Zealand ambassador to the UN).
40. Matheson, *Council Unbound*, p. 24.
41. Matheson, p. 24.
42. Matheson, pp. 26–31.
43. UN Security Council, Resolution 1970, S/RES/1970, paras. 9, 10, 15, 17 (Feb. 26, 2011). The Security Council established a Committee Concerning Libya, which originally passed a series of resolutions imposing an arms embargo, assets freeze, travel bans, and, then, in UN Security Council, Resolution 2009, S/RES/2009, paras. 13–21 (Sept. 16, 2011), eased some restrictions and in UN Security Council, Resolution 2016, S/RES/2016, para. 6 (Oct. 27, 2011), lifted the no-fly zone. The procedural maneuver the committee used was to issue resolutions that did not overturn previous ones but sufficiently limited their effect in order to allow for financial and arms assistance to reach Libya after the transition to the new government.
44. Matheson, *Council Unbound*, p. 30: "One striking aspect of all these delegations of decision-making authority is that the process by which decisions are made by these bodies varies considerably and in no instance conforms to the voting rules of Article 27 of the Charter." UN Charter, Art. 27, para. 1.
45. Anna Spain, "The U.N. Security Council's Duty to Decide," *Harvard National Security Journal* 4, no. 2 (2013), 333–4.
46. Spain, 333–4.
47. UN Security Council, Resolution 1973, S/RES/1973, para. 4 (March 17, 2011), https://undocs.org/S/RES/1973(2011): "*Authorizes* Member States that have notified the Secretary-General, acting nationally or through regional organizations or arrangements, and acting in cooperation with the Secretary-General, to take all necessary measures, notwithstanding paragraph 9 of resolution 1970 (2011), to protect civilians and civilian populated areas under threat of attack in the Libyan Arab Jamahiriya, including Benghazi, while excluding a foreign occupation force of any form on any part of Libyan territory, and *requests* the Member States concerned to inform the Secretary-General immediately of the measures they take pursuant to the authorization conferred by this paragraph which shall be immediately reported to the Security Council"; S/RES/1973, ¶7: "Reiterating the responsibility of the Libyan authorities to protect the Libyan population and reaffirming that parties to armed conflicts bear the primary responsibility to take all feasible steps to ensure the protection of civilians."
48. UN Security Council, Resolution 1970, S/RES/1970, paras. 9, 10, 15, 17 (Feb. 26, 2011). The Security Council established a Committee Concerning Libya, which originally passed a series of resolutions imposing an arms embargo, assets freeze, travel bans, and then, in UN Security Council, Resolution 2009, S/RES/2009, paras. 13–21 (Sept. 16,

2011), eased some restrictions. UN Security Council, Resolution 2016, S/RES/2016, para. 6 (Oct. 27, 2011), lifted the no-fly zone. The procedural maneuver the committee used was to issue resolutions that did not overturn previous ones but sufficiently limited their effect in order to allow for financial and arms assistance to reach Libya after the transition to the new government.

49. Anna Spain, "Deciding to Intervene," *Houston Law Review* 51, no. 847 (2014).

50. The resolution also required member states to notify UN Secretary General Ban Ki-moon and Arab League Secretary General Amr Moussa of their plans prior to acting.

51. The Responsibility to Protect, Report of the International Commission on Intervention and State Sovereignty (2001), http://responsibilitytoprotect .org/ICISS%20Report.pdf. Gareth Evans, "Responsibility to Protect (R2P): The ICISS Commission Fifteen Years On," *Simon Papers in Security and Development*, no. 54/2016 (2016); High-Level Panel on Threats, Challenges and Change, A More Secure World: Our Shared Responsibility: Report of the High-Level Panel on Threats, Challenges and Change, A/59/565, ¶29 (Dec. 2, 2004); UN General Assembly, 2005 World Summit Outcome, GA Res. 60/1, para. 138–139 (Oct. 24, 2005).

52. "Gaddafi Speech was 'Code to Begin Genocide Against Libyans,'" *The Telegraph*, February 23, 2011, www.telegraph.co.uk/news/worldnews/afri caandindianocean/libya/8342349/Gaddafi-speech-was-code-to-begin-gen ocide-against-Libyans.html (Report by Mr. Dabbashi, Deputy Ambassador, Libyan Mission to the United Nations, (Feb. 23, 2011)).

53. Shadi Hamid, "Everyone Says the Libya Intervention was a Failure. They're Wrong," Brookings, April 12, 2016, www.brookings.edu/blog/mar kaz/2016/04/12/everyone-says-the-libya-intervention-was-a-failure-theyre-w rong/; see, also Shirin Tahir-Kheli, "UN Security Council Vote on Libya: Why BRIC Countries Abstained," *Daily Beast*, March 19, 2011, www .thedailybeast.com/un-security-council-vote-on-libya-why-bric-countries-abstained (Shiring Tahir-Kheli is a former US ambassador to the UN for special political affairs and former special assistant to the US president and senior director for democracy, human rights, and international operations at the National Security Council, the White House).

54. Helene Cooper and Steven Lee Myers, "Obama Takes Hard Line With Libya After Shift by Clinton," *NYT* (March 18, 2011). Cf. interview with Catherine Powell, who served as senior advisor, US State Department, Secretary of State's Policy Planning Office and describes the intensity of this moment noting the administration's sense that "the world could not look away as it did in Rwanda," and the team's sense of "personal obligation and responsibility" (June 26, 2020). See Catherine Powell, "Libya: A Multilateral Constitutional Moment?" *American Journal of International Law* 106 (2012): 298–316.

55. NATO to conduct air strikes. China and Russia abstained but did not veto. Air strikes stopped the tanks. NATO planes helped protestors attack government forces and the result of an overthrow of Qaddafi's regime. NATO went beyond its mandate?

56. See, for example, Tim Gaynor and Tahah Zargoun, "Gaddafi Caught like 'Rat' in a Drain, Humiliated and Shot, *Reuters*, October 21, 2011, www .reuters.com/article/us-libya-gaddafi-finalhours-idUSTRE79K43S20111021.

57. Interview with Person R (August 16, 2017).

58. Interview with R.

59. International Criminal Court, Situation in Libya referred to the ICC by the United Nations Security Council (March 2011), www.icc-cpi.int/libya.

60. Interview with R (noting unconfirmed rumors that the Russian prime minister did not want to exercise the veto).

61. S/RES/1973, para. 4.

62. Interview with R.

63. Fasulo, *An Insider's Guide to the UN*, p. 64.

64. Alexander L. George, "The Case for Multiple Advocacy in Making Foreign Policy," *American Political Science Review* 66, no. 3 (1972); Robert Jervice, *Perception and Misperception in International Politics* (Princeton, NJ: Princeton University Press, 1976); Margaret G. Hermann, "Explaining Foreign Policy Behavior Using Personal Characteristics of Political Leaders," *International Studies Quarterly* 24, no. 1 (1980).

65. Theories of personality in psychology: Keren Yarhi-Milo, *Who Fights for Reputation: The Psychology of Leaders in International Conflict* (Princeton, NJ: Princeton University Press, 2018), p. 3: "Dispositions or psychological traits of individuals significantly shape their understanding of 'the logic of images' in international relations."; Leonie Huddy, David O. Sears, and Jack S. Levy, eds., *The Handbook of Political Psychology*, 2nd ed. (Oxford: Oxford University Press, 2013); Philip E. Tetlock, "Cognitive Style and Political Ideology," *Journal of Personality and Social Psychology* 45, no. 1 (1983); Margaret G. Hermann, "Assessing Leadership Style: A Trait Analysis," *in The Psychological Assessment of Political Leaders*, ed. Jerrold Post (Ann Arbor, MI: University of Michigan Press, 2005), pp. 178–214; Hermann, "Explaining Foreign Policy Behavior Using Personal Characteristics of Political Leaders."

66. Janis, *Groupthink*, p. 13.

67. Decision errors occur for various psychological reasons and because of failures in process, when no one questions underlying assumptions or offers dissent. The group takes on a life bigger than that of any one individual, and group cohesion becomes valued more than accurate information or high-quality analysis. See Sandeep Baliga and Tomas Sjöström, "The Hobbesian Trap," in *The Oxford Handbook Of The Economics Of Peace And Conflict*, eds. Michelle R. Garfinkel and

Stergious Skaperdas (Oxford: Oxford University Press, 2012), pp. 93–6, 106–7 (describing the Hobbesian Trap as caused by a "fear spiral" that will promote the inclination).

68. Madeline Albright, "On being a Woman and a Diplomat," Interview by Pat Mitchell, TEDWomen 2010, December, 2010, www.ted.com/talks/ madeleine_albright_on_being_a_woman_and_a_diplomat#t-5796.

69. Leticia Marquez, "10 Questions for Kantathi Suphamongkhon on His Diplomatic Career and Lessons Learned from Nixon," UCLA Today, January 19, 2011, www.international.ucla.edu/asia/article/119600.

70. *Merriam-Webster*, s.v. "trust (*n.*)," accessed January 14, 2020, www .merriam-webster.com/dictionary/trust.

71. Paul J. Zak, *Trust Factor: The Science of Creating High-Performance Companies* (New York: AMACOM, 2017), pp. 2–7.

72. Zak, *Trust Factor*, p. 7.

73. Interview with R.

74. See, for example, Howard Gardner, *Changing Minds: The Art and Science of Changing Our Own and Other People's Minds* (Boston, MA: Harvard Business Review Press, 2006).

75. Interview with R.

76. Kahneman, *Thinking Fast and Slow*, pp. 79–88 (describing heuristics as a "machine for jumping to conclusions" that lead to overconfidence, framing effects, base-rate neglect and other cognitive biases); Shelley E. Taylor, "The Availability Bias in Social Perception and Interaction," in *Judgment Under Uncertainty*, pp. 190–1 (explaining the meaning of "satisfice"); Dixon and Ginsburg, "Deciding Not to Decide," 639: "When the stakes are high, there is naturally some reluctance to making the wrong decision too early; when stakes are low but the probability of error is high, deferral also makes sense as a strategy." Sunstein and Thaler, *Nudge*, p. 8.

77. Cognitive functioning in decision making has been tested through a variety of means. See, for example, Vartanian and Mandel, "Introduction," in *The Neuroscience of Decisionmaking*, p. 2 (describing why cognition is not easily defined as automatic vs. non-automatic as many processes feature some aspects of both); Jan De Houwer and Dirk Hermans, "Do Feelings Have a Mind of Their Own?" in *Cognition and Emotion: Reviews of Current Research and Theories*, eds. Jan De Houwer and Dirk Hermans (New York: Psychology Press, 2010), p. 44: "Evidence from Stroop studies, for instance, suggests that the processing of word meaning is automatic in that it does not depend on intention, resources or time, but at the same time occurs only when attention is directed toward the word (See Logan, 1985, 1989,

for reviews). An important implication of this conclusion is that one cannot simply characterize a process as automatic or non-automatic."

78. Houwer and Hermans, "Do Feelings Have a Mind of Their Own?" 7 ("affective reactions can occur independently of controlled cognition"); J.H. Song and K. Nakayama, "Hidden Cognitive States Revealed in Choice Reaching Tasks," *Trends in Cognitive Sciences* 13, no. 8 (2009), 360. For studies investigating parallel cognitive processes, see M. J. Spivey et al., "Do Curved Reaching Movements Emerge From Competing Perception?" *Journal of Experimental Psychology: Human Perception and Performance* 26, no. 1 (2009), 251, https://somby .ceu.edu/sites/somby.ceu.edu/files/attachment/basicpage/6/2010spivey .pdf ("existence proof that a discrete-processing speech perception system can feed into a continuous- processing motor movement system to produce reach trajectories"); Alon Fishback and F.A. Mussa-Ivaldi, "Seeing vs. Believing: Conflicting Immediate and Predicted Feedback Lead to Sub-Optimal Motor Performance," *Journal of Neuroscience* 28 (2008), 14140: "Under normal conditions, perceptual and motor criteria for movement optimization coincide. However, when vision is perturbed adapted trajectories can be used to uncover the influence of perceptual criteria on movement planning"; Hongbao Li et al., "Prior Knowledge of Target Direction and Intended Movement Selection Improves Indirect Reaching Movement Decoding," *Behavioral Neurology* (2017), Abstract: "Recruiting prior knowledge about target direction and intended movement selection extracted from the Dorsal Pre-Motor Cortex could enhance the decoding performance of hand trajectory in indirect reaching movement."

79. Through these varied methodologies, scientists can measure neural networks and systems in addition to neural functions. See, for example, John P. O' Doherty and Peter Bossaerts, "Toward a Mechanistic Understanding of Human Decision Making: Contributions of Functional Neuroimaging," *Current Directions in Psychological Science* 17, no. 2 (2008); Brian Knutson et al., "Distributed Neural Representation of Expected Value," *Journal of Neuroscience* 25, no. 19 (2005).

80. See, for example, Bechara et al., "Different Contributions of the Human Amygdala, (discussing how the ventromedial prefrontal cortex and the amygdala affect different processes); Valeria Gazzola, Lisa Aziz-Zade, and Christian Keysers , "Empathy and the Somatotopic Auditory Mirror System in Humans," *Current Biology* 16, no. 18 (2006). A 2013 study found that emotions generated from observing a film increased neural activity in the medial prefrontal cortex, the thalamus, and other emotion centers of the brain. But, instead of triggering parts of the brain associated with pain, the observation triggered the brain's center for

processing emotional content. Watson and Greenberg, "Empathetic Resonance," 127–8.

81. President Bill Clinton, interview on Rwandan Genocide, CNBC News (2003).

82. See, for example, Matheson, *Council Unbound.*

83. Interview with UN Security Council official, November 1, 2013 (on file with author). The source wishes to remain anonymous.

84. S/RES/1973, para. 4: "Authorizes Member States that have notified the Secretary–General, acting nationally or through regional organizations or arrangements, and acting in cooperation with the Secretary–General, to take all necessary measures, notwithstanding paragraph 9 of resolution 1970 (2011), to protect civilians and civilian populated areas under threat of attack." See President Barack Obama, "Remarks at Joint Press Conference," March 3, 2011, www.whitehouse.gov/the-press- office/2011/03/28/remarks-president-address-nation-libya ("Qaddafi had lost the confidence of his people and the legitimacy to lead, and I said that he needed to step down from power"); Ethan Bronner and David E. Sanger, "No-Flight Zone in Libya Backed by Arab League," *New York Times*, March 13, 2011. The endorsement by the Arab League of a no-fly zone was significant because they were willing to allow a foreign military presence capable of enforcement. Bronner and Sanger.

85. Interview with UN Security Council official.

86. Kofi Annan, "*We the Peoples: The Role of the United Nations in the 21st Century*," (New York: United Nations, 2000), p. 48, www.un.org/en/events/pastevents/pdfs/We_The_Peoples.pdf.

87. Jean-Marc de La Sablière, former permanent representative of France to the UN, and first chair of the Security Council Working Group on Children and Armed Conflict: "The children and armed conflict mandate has been used as a model for the question of protection of civilians and has influenced the development of other mandates related to the protection of civilians. This mandate must be considered a success story for the United Nations."

88. Lloyd Axworthy, "The Protection of Civilians in Armed Conflict," Notes for an address to the UNSC, New York, (Feb. 12, 1999, reprinted in DFAIT, Statements and Speeches 1999, p. 1).

89. UN Security Council, Resolution 815, S/RES/815 (March 30, 1993).

90. Interview with R.

91. Interview with UN Security Council official.

92. Interview with R.

6 HUMAN CHOICE IN HUMAN RIGHTS

1. Leymah Gbowee (with Carol Mithers), *Mighty Be Our Powers: How Sisterhood, Prayer, and Sex Changed a Nation at War: A Memoir* (Beast Books, 2011), p. 173.
2. UN Office of the Special Representative of the Secretary-General for Children and Armed Conflict. "Voice from the Field," www .youtube.com/watch?v=kJSBH-GKQs.
3. UN Office of the Special Representative of the Secretary-General for Children and Armed Conflict. "Voice from the Field," https://vimeo .com/122956351.
4. For context, see Mark Drumbl, *Reimagining Child Soldiers in International Law and Policy* (Oxford: Oxford University Press, 2012).
5. Saira Mohammed, "Of Monsters and Men: Perpetrator Trauma and Mass Atrocity," 115 *Columbia Law Review* 1157 (2015); Saira Mohammed, "Deviance, Aspiration, and the Stories We Tell: Reconciling Mass Atrocity and the Criminal Law," 124 *Yale Law Journal* 1628 (2015); Laurel Fletcher, "Refracted Justice: The Imagined Victim and the International Criminal Court," in *Contested Justice: the Politics and Practice of International Criminal Court Interventions*, eds. C.M. De Vos, Sara Kendall, and Carsten Stahn (Cambridge: Cambridge University Press, 2015) p. 302; James E. Waller, *Becoming Evil: How Ordinary People Commit Genocide and Mass Killings* (Oxford: Oxford University Press, 2002).
6. Michael Zürn and Monika Heupel, eds., *An Introduction in Protecting the Individual from International Authority: Human Rights Protection in International Organizations* (Cambridge: Cambridge University Press, 2017), p. 4.
7. See, for example, S. Langdon and Alan H. Gardiner, "The Treaty of Alliance between Hattusili, King of the Hittites, and the Pharaoh Ramesses II of Egypt," *The Journal of Egyptian Archaeology* 6, no. 3(July 1920); Aristide Theodorides, "The Concept of Law in Ancient Egypt," in *The Legacy of Egypt*, 2nd ed., ed. J.R. Harris (Oxford: Oxford University Press, 1971), p. 291; J.G. Manning, "The Representation of Justice in Ancient Egypt," *Yale Journal of Law and Humanities* 24, no. 1 (January 2012).
8. Adolf Berger, *Encyclopedic Dictionary of Roman Law*, vol. 43, bk. 2 (Philadelphia, PA: American Philosophical Society,1953) (defined as "the human tendency as an ethical commandment, benevolent consideration for others).
9. Hugo Grotius, *De Jure Belli AC Pacis* (1625), trans. Francis W. Kelsey (Oxford: Oxford University Press, 1925), p. 55: "The disputes arising from those who are held together by no common bond of civil laws to decide

their dissensions, who formed no national community, or the numerous unconnected communities ... all bear a relation to the circumstances of war and peace." See, also, Hersch Lauterpacht, "The Grotian Tradition in International Law," *British Yearbook of International Law* 23 (1946). Grotius, *De Jure Belli*, p. 35. See, generally, Martin Van Gelderen , "The Challenges of Colonialism: Grotius and Vitoria on Natural Law and International Law," *Grotiana* 14, no. 1 (1993); Richard Falk, Friedrich Kratochwil, and Saul H. Mendlovitz, eds., *International Law: A Contemporary Perspective* (Boulder, CO: Westview Press, 1985), p. 7. See Boutros Boutros-Ghali, "A Grotian Moment," *Fordham International Law Journal* 18, no. 5 (1994); Richard Truck, *The Rights of War and Peace: Political Thought and the International Order from Grotius to Kant* (Oxford: Oxford University Press, 1999); B.S. Chimni, "A Just World Under Law: A View from the South," *American University International Law Review* 22, no. 2 (2007), 202; Michael P. Scharf, "Seizing the 'Grotian Moment': Accelerated Formation of Customary International Law in Times of Change," *Cornell International Law Journal* 43, no. 3 (2010).

10. The Declaration of Independence (USA 1776); The Declaration of the Rights of Man and Citizen (France 1789). These documents and the new governments that sprung from them did little for the rights of the millions of enslaved women, men, and children or oppressed indigenous peoples deemed racially inferior and unworthy of such inherent rights.

11. *Encyclopedia Britannica Online*, s.v. "The Haitian Revolution," accessed February 9, 2019, www.britannica.com/topic/Haitian-Revolution [https://perma.cc/33CC-7EPP].

12. Act Prohibiting Importation of Slaves, 2 Stat. 426 (1807); Abolition of the Slave Trade Act 1807, 47 and 48 Geo. 3 (UK). Jenny S. Martinez, *The Slave Trade and the Origins of International Human Rights Law* (Oxford: Oxford University Press, 2012) (demonstrating how tribunals set up in Cuba, Brazil and Sierra Leone during the slave trade formed the first international adjudicative bodies designed to hear human rights cases); Anna Spain Bradley, "Human Rights Racism," *Harvard Human Rights Journal* 32, no. 1 (2019) (providing an inclusive history of human rights and international law).

13. International Covenant on Civil and Political Rights (ICCPR), 1966, 999 UNTS 171; International Covenant on Economic, Social and Cultural Rights (ICESCR), 1966, 993 UNTS 3; Convention on the Elimination of All Forms of Discrimination Against Women (CEDAW), 1979, 1249 UNTS 13.

14. U Thant, Portfolio for Peace: Excerpts from the Writings and Speeches of U Thant, *Secretary-General of the United Nations, on Major World Issues 1961–1968* (New York: United Nations, 1968) p. 92.

15. Henry J. Richardson III, "Two Treaties, and Global Influence of the American Civil Rights Movement, Through the Black International Tradition," 18 *Va. J. Soc. Pol. & L.* 1 (2010), 75–6. Henry J. *Richardson III, The Origins of the African-American Interests in International Law* (Durham, NC: Carolina Academic Press, 2008).
16. Application of the Convention on the Prevention and Punishment of the Crime of Genocide (*The Gambia* v. *Myanmar*) (November 11, 2019).
17. Makau Mutua, *Human Rights, A Political and Cultural Critique* (Philadelphia, PA: Penn University Press, 2008).
18. For a list of international human rights' courts, tribunals and institutions, see Gerd Oberleitner, ed., *International Human Rights Institutions, Tribunals, and Courts* (New York: Springer, 2018); Stefan Kadelbach, Thilo Rensmann, and Eva Reiter, eds., *Judging International Human Rights, Courts of General Jurisdiction as Human Rights Courts* (New York: Springer, 2019).
19. "Composition of the Court," European Court of Human Rights, last updated January 1, 2020, https://echr.coe.int/Pages/home.aspx?p=court/ judges&c=#n1368718271710_pointer.
20. See, for example, Council of Europe, Annual Report 2019 of the European Court of Human Rights, https://echr.coe.int/Documents/Ann ual_report_2019_ENG.pdf; *Chiragov* v. *Armenia*, App. No. 13216/05, ECtHR (2015); *Sargsyan* v. *Azerbaijan*, App. No. 40167/06, ECtHR (2011); *Georgia* v. *Russia* (I), App. No. 13255/07, ECtHR (2009).
21. See UN Security Council Resolutions 1267, S/RES/1267 (Oct. 15, 1999); 1333, S/RES/1333 (Dec. 19, 2000); 1363, S/RES/1363 (July 30, 2001); 1388, S/ RES/1388 (Jan. 15, 2002); 1390, S/RES/1390 (Jan. 16, 2002); 1452, S/RES/1452 (Dec. 20, 2002); 1455, S/RES/1455 (Jan. 17, 2003), 1456, S/RES/1456 (Jan. 20, 2003); 1526, S/RES/1526 (Jan. 30, 2004); 1617, S/RES/1617 (July 29, 2005); 1699, S/RES/1699 (Aug. 8, 2006); 1730, S/RES/1730 (Dec. 19, 2006); 1732, S/ RES/1732 (Dec. 21, 2006); 1735, S/RES/1735 (Dec. 22, 2006).
22. Case C–402/05 P and C–415/05, P. *Kadi and Al Barakaat International Foundation* v. *Council and Commission* [2008] ECR I–6351, https://eur-lex.europa.eu/legal-content/EN/TXT/HTML/?uri=CELEX:62005 CJ0402&from=EN.
23. *Kadi and Al Barakaat*, Opinion of AG Poiares Maduro, para. 54.
24. She is the youngest daughter of Aung San, Father of the Nation. She won the Nobel Peace Prize in 1991 and was under house arrest from 1989–2010 as a political prisoner. In December of 2019, she appeared before the International Court of Justice defending Myanmar against allegations of genocide against the Rohingya people brought by The Gambia.
25. See generally, Se-shauna Wheatle, *Principled Reasoning in Human Rights Adjudication* (Oxford: Hart Publishing, 2017).
26. UN Security Council, Resolution 1325, S/RES/1325 (Oct. 31, 2000).

27. Statement by the President of the Security Council, UN SCOR, S/PRST/2006/28 (June 22, 2006).

28. Heupel and Zürn, *Protecting the Individual*, p. 5. Declaration of the High-level Meeting of the General Assembly on the Rule of Law at the National and International Levels, GA Res. 1, UN Doc. A/67/L.1 (Sept. 19, 2012), adopted as UN Doc. A/RES/67/1 (Sept. 24, 2012).

29. "Introduction," HR Commission Archives, United Nations Human Rights Council, accessed April 20,2020, www.ohchr.org/en/hrbodies/chr/pages/commissiononhumanrights.aspx

30. Richard Goldstone et al., Human Rights in Palestine and Other Occupied Arab Territories: Report of the United Nations Fact-Finding Mission on the Gaza Conflict, UN GAOR, 12th sess., Agenda Item 7, UN Doc A/HRC/12/48 (Sept. 25, 2009) ("Goldstone Report").

31. Human Rights Council, GA Res. 251, UN GAOR, UN Doc. A/RES/60/251 (March 15, 2006). The council is composed of forty-seven UN member states elected by the UN General Assembly.

32. Krishnadev Calamur, "The UN Human Rights Council Is a Deeply Flawed Body," *The Atlantic*, June 20, 2018, www.theatlantic.com/international/archive/2018/06/us-un-human-rights/563276/.

33. ICERD, Thornberry.

34. UN Charter, Art. 1.3, Art. 55 (1945).

35. *A.T.* v. *Hungary*, Comm. 2/2003, UN Doc. CEDAW/C/36/D/2/2003 (2005).

36. Thomas Franck, "Are Human Rights Universal?" *Foreign Affairs* (Jan/Feb 2001); Raimon Panikkar and Arvind Sharma, *Human Rights as a Western Concept* (D.K. Printworld, 2007); Makau Mutua, *Human Rights Standards: Hegemony, Law and Politics* (2016).

37. John Wendle, "The Aisha Bibi Case: Her Father Wants to Petition the Taliban for Justice," *Time* (July 14, 2011).

38. W.E.B. DuBois and the NAACP, A Statement on the Denial of Human Rights Minorities in the Case of Citizens of Negro Descent in the U.S.A. and an Appeal to the United Nations for Redress (Oct. 23, 1947), www.aclu.org/appeal-world [https://perma.cc/PWG3-SK3V]; Henry J. Richardson, "Dr. Martin Luther King, Jr. as an International Human Rights Leader," 52 *Vill. L. Rev.* (2007), 471, 473–5 (recalling the history of the "Black International Tradition" and the efforts of W.E.B. DuBois, the NAACP, Thurgood Marshall, Dr. Martin Luther King Jr., and other civil rights leaders in shaping international human rights and the creation of the United Nations); Carol Anderson, "Eyes Off the Prize: The United Nations and the African-American Struggle for Human Rights, 1944–1955" 108 (2003); Anna Spain Bradley, "Human Rights Racism," *Harvard Human Rights Journal* 32 (2019).

39. International Convention on the Elimination of All Forms of Racial Discrimination, Dec. 21, 1965, TIAS94–1120 (hereafter ICERD), Art. 3.

40. Oral hearings in ICJ Advisory Opinion on the Threat or Use of Nuclear Weapons.

41. African Group before the Human Rights Council calling for urgent debate on systemic racial discrimination in the USA and beyond, 2020.

42. Inter-American Court of Human Rights, www.corteidh.or.cr/index-en.cfm.

43. *Atala Riffo and Daughters* v. *Chile*, Merits, Reparations, and Costs, Judgment Inter-Am. Ct. HR (ser. C) No. 239, para. 30 (Feb. 24, 2012).

44. *Atala Riffo and Daughters* v. *Chile*, Judgement paras. 83–93.

45. Alvaro Paul, "Examining Atala-Riffo and Daughters v. Chile, the First Inter-American Case on Sexual Orientation, and some of its Implications," 7 *Inter-American and European Human R. J.* (2014), 54–74.

46. Jorge Contesse, "Settling Human Rights Violations," *Harvard International Law Journal* 60, no. 2 (2019), 318–19.

47. "November 2018 Hearing Schedule," Inter-American Court of Human Rights, www.oas.org/en/iachr/sessions/docs/Calendario-169-audiencias-en.pdf.

48. In other words, there is no single controlling definition of empathy from a neuroscientific perspective. See Batson, "These Things Called Empathy," 3–15 (describing eight concepts for understanding the phenomenon of one person's caring response to another's suffering). Wagner, Handke, and Walter, "The Relationship Between Trait Empathy and Memory Formation," 1; see also Clifford B. Saper, 'The Central Autonomic Nervous System: Conscious Visceral Perception and Autonomic Pattern Generation," *Annual Review of Neuroscience* 25 (2002), 453–61 (describing patterns of autonomic responses in the central nervous system); Kevin A. Keay and Richard Bandler, "Parallel Circuits Mediating Distinct Emotional Coping Reactions to Different Types of Stress," *Neuroscience & Biobehavioral Reviews* 25, no. 7–8 (2001), 669 (establishing that emotional coping strategies to different types of stress arise through distinct, longitudinal neuronal columns of the midbrain periaqueductal gray (PAG) region). McClure et al., "Conflict Monitoring Cognition-Emotion Competition."
See Wagner, Handke, and Walter, "The Relationship Between Trait Empathy and Memory Formation," 7 (refuting earlier studies arguing empathy is innate); see, for example, Jean Decety and Philip L. Jackson, "The Functional Architecture of Human Empathy," *Behavioral and Cognitive Neuroscience Reviews* 3, no. 2 (2004), 73–5 (proposing empathy as an "innate ability to recognize that the self and the other can be the same"); and Greenberg, "Empathetic Resonance: A Neuroscience Perspective," 126.

49. Christian Keysers, Netherlands Institute for Neuroscience, Amsterdam: "When we witness what happens to others, we don't just activate the visual cortex like we thought some decades ago, ... we also activate our own actions as if we'd be acting in similar ways. We activate our own emotions and sensations as if we felt the same"; www.psychologicalscience.org/observer/i-feel-your-pain-the-neuroscience-of-empathy.

50. Neil R. Carlson, *Foundations of Behavioral Neuroscience*, 9th ed. (Boston, MA: Pearson Education Inc., 2014), p. 245.

51. Carlson, *Foundations*, p. 245.

52. Research in this area has focused primarily on negative emotions such as fear and anger. Research concerning the influence and operation of positive emotion is emergent.

53. Carlson, *Foundations*, p. 422: "physiological reaction caused by the perception of aversive or threatening situations."

54. Carlson, pp. 423–4.

55. Carlson, p. 423.

56. CEDAW (1979).

57. 39 UN GAOR 2 Supp. (No. 45) para. 109, UN Doc. A/39/45 (1984), as cited in Theodor Meron, *Human Rights Law-Making in the United Nations* (Oxford: Clarendon Press, 1986), p. 56.

58. Fasulo, *An Insider's Guide to the UN*, pp. 255–6.

59. Fasulo, pp. 254.

7 CHANGING THE CULTURE OF CHOICE

1. "To cite a quote from this book, more of us understand that 'we are linked, not ranked'." Gloria Steinem, *The Truth Will Set You Free, but First It Will Piss You Off* (New York: Random House Publishing, 2019), p. xx.

2. *Case Concerning Armed Activities*; Convention on the Prevention and Punishment of the Crime of Genocide, Dec. 9, 1948, UNTS 78.

3. I have expressed this view before. Anna Spain, "Mock Debate Remarks: Is the Primacy of the ICJ in International Dispute Settlement Under Threat?" (panel speaker), April 1, 2016, American Society of International Law 110th Annual Meeting, video and audio, www.youtube.com/watch?v=hnfhHvPdnp c. See also Chester Brown, "*Mock Debate: Is the Primacy of the ICJ in International Dispute Settlement in Under Threat?*" in *Proceedings: ASIL Proceedings of the 110th Annual Meeting* (Cambridge: Cambridge University Press, 2016), pp. 191–6. Anna Spain, "Examining the International Judicial Function: International Courts as Dispute Resolvers," 34 *Loyola of Los Angeles International and Comparative Law Review* 5–31 (2011, symposium edition).

4. *Case Concerning Armed Activities*, Joint Separate Opinion of Judges Higgins, Kooijmans, Elaraby, Owada, and Simma p. 71.

5. David D. Caron, Remarks, The Charles N. Brower Lecture on International Dispute Resolution (April 14, 2017).

6. David D. Caron, Towards a Political Theory of International Courts and Tribunals, 24 *Berk. J. Int'l L.* 401 (2006).

7. Kaitlin Ugolik Phillips, *The Future of Feeling* (New York: A. Little Publishers, 2020); Brene Brown, *Daring Greatly: How the Courage to Be Vulnerable Transforms the Way We Live, Love, Parent and Lead* (New York: Avery Press, 2012).

8. Simon Sinek, *Leaders Eat Last: Why Some Teams Pull Together and Others Don't* (New York: Penguin Random House, 2014).

9. Michael Brenner, *Mean People Suck: How Empathy Leads to Bigger Profits and a Better Life* (Westchester, PA: Marketing Insider Publishing, 2019).

10. Kaitlin Ugolik Phillips, *The Future of Feeling* (New York: Little A., 2020); Brene Brown, *Daring Greatly: How the Courage to Be Vulnerable Transforms the Way We Live, Love, Parent, and Lead* (New York: Gotham Books, 2012).

8 THE INTERNATIONAL LAW WE NEED

1. Nikos Kazantzakis, *Report to Greco* (New York: Simon & Schuster, 1965), p. 434.

2. Cass Sunstein, *How Change Happens* (Cambridge: MIT Press, 2019), p. 3: "[w]hen norms start to collapse, people are unleashed."

3. *The Puzzle of Peace: The Evolution of Peace in the International System*, Gary Goertz, Paul F. Diehl, and Alexandru Balas eds., Oxford, New York: Oxford University Press, 2016. Steven Pinker, *The Better Angels of Our Nature, Why Violence has Declined* (2011), p. xxi: "[V]iolence has declined over long stretches of time, and today we may be living in the most peaceable era in our species' existence." Joshua Goldstein, *Winning the War on War: The Decline of Armed Conflict Worldwide* 2011). See Uppsala Conflict Data Program (2014), at http://ucdp.uu.se (providing data sets on the number of conflicts 1975–2015, number of deaths per conflict 1989–2015, and more).

4. Joel P. Trachtman, *The Future of International Law: Global Government* (Cambridge: Cambridge University Press, 2013).

5. Legality of the Threat or Use of Nuclear Weapons, Dissenting Opinion of Vice President Schwebel, ICJ Rep. 1996, p. 311.

6. UN Charter, Preamble.

7. As Chapter 2 explored, there are numerous ways to understand what international law is and how it works alongside concerns that the field and our understandings of it are too vast. See Statute of the International Court of Justice, art. 38; Andrea Bianchi, *International Law Theories: An*

Inquiry Into Different Ways of Thinking (Oxford: Oxford University Press, 2016); Jean d' Aspremont, *International Law as a Belief System* (Cambridge: Cambridge University Press, 2017). But see International Law Commission, *Fragmentation of International Law: Difficulties Arising from the Diversification and Expansion of International Law — Report of the Study Group of the International Law Commission* UN Doc. A/CN.4/L.682 (Apr. 13, 2006), as corrected UN Doc. A/CN.4/L.682/Corr.1 (Aug. 11, 2006) (finalized by Martti Koskenniemi).

8. Samantha Besson, Max Planck Encyclopedia of International Law (April 2011), https://opil.ouplaw.com/view/10.1093/law:epil/9780199923169 0/law-9780199231690-e1472.

9. Oppenheim, *International Law*, p. 18.

10. Reparation for Injuries Suffered in the Service of the United Nations, Advisory Opinion, 1949 ICJ Rep. 149 (Apr. 11).

11. For a history of the development of *jus gentium* in international law, see Antônio Augusto Cançado Trindade, *International Law for Humankind: Towards a New Jus Gentium, General Course on Public International Law* (Hague Academy of International Law, 2006) pp. 37–60.

12. *Oxford Bibliographies Online*, s.v. "Jus Cogens," by Anne Lagerwall, last reviewed Nov. 7, 2017, www.oxfordbibliographies.com/view/document/obo-9780199796953/obo-9780199796953–0124.xml; Robert Kolb, *Théorie du Ius Cogens International: Essai de Relecture du Concept* (Paris: Presses Universitaires de France, 2001); Christian Tomuschat and Jean-Marc Thouvenin, eds., *The Fundamental Rules of the International Legal Order* (Leiden, The Netherlands: Martinus Nijhoff, 2006); Alexander Orakhelashvili, *Peremptory Norms in International Law* (Oxford: Oxford University Press, 2006).

13. Jochen A. Frowein, "Obligations erga omnes," *in Max Planck Encyclopedia of Public International Law* (Oxford: Oxford University Press, 2008), https://opil.ouplaw.com/view/10.1093/law:epil/9780199923169 0/law-9780199231690-e1400.

14. "The ICJ has confirmed the existence of obligations *erga omnes* in *East Timor (Portugal v Australia)* ('*East Timor Case*' para. 29); and in *Legal Consequences of the Construction of a Wall in the Occupied Palestinian Territory (Advisory Opinion)* paras 155–60)." Frowein, "Obligations erga omnes."

15. Antonio Cassese, "*Soliloquy*," *The Human Dimension of International Law* (Oxford: Oxford University Press, 2008) p. lxxvi. Oppenheim, *International Law*, p. 637: "It is quite correct to say that individuals have these rights in conformity with, or according to, International Law, provided it is remembered that, as a rule, these rights would not be enforceable before national courts had the several States not created them by their Municipal Law."

16. Robert Y. Jennings, "The Role of the International Court of Justice," *British Yearbook of International Law* 68, no. 1 (1997), 58.

17. Robert Y. Jennings, "An International Lawyer Takes Stock," *International and Comparative Law Quarterly* 39, no. 3 (1990), 522.

18. Antonio Cassese, *The Human Dimension of International Law* (Oxford: Oxford University Press, 2008).

19. Meron, *The Humanization of International Law*, p. 1.

20. Lieber Code (1863); Hague Convention (II) respecting the Laws and Customs of War on Land, and Annex, opened for signature July 29, 1899, 32 Stat. 1803, 1805; Hague Convention (IV) respecting the Laws and Customs of War on Land, and Annex, *opened for signature* Oct. 18 1907, 36 Stat. 2277, 2279–80.

21. Meron, *The Humanization of International Law*, p. 11.

22. Universal Declaration of Human Rights.

23. UNDHR, Art. 20.

24. Dinah Shelton, *The Oxford Handbook of International Human Rights Law* (Oxford University Press: Oxford, 2013), p. 2.

25. Teitel, *Humanity's Law*, p. 4.

26. Fiona McKay, "What Outcomes for Victims," in *Oxford Handbook of International Human Rights*, pp. 921–54; Penny Miles, "Challenging Heteronormativity: Atala Riffo and daughters v. Chile," in S. Smart, K. Fernandez, and C. Pena eds., *Chile and the Inter-American Human Rights System* (2017), pp. 65, 74 (Rosa M. Celorio, The Case of Karen Atala and Daughters: Toward a Better Understanding of Discrimination, Equality, and the Rights of Women, 15 *CUNY L. Rev.* 335 (2012), 340. Kofi Oteng Kufuor, *The African Human Rights System: Origin and Evolution* 133–38 (2010). Anton Bosl and Joseph Diescho, eds., *Human Rights in Africa: Legal Perspectives on Their Protection and Promotion* (2009), pp. 233, 265. Dilek Kurban, Forsaking Individual Justice: The Implications of the European Court of Human Rights' Pilot Judgment Procedure for Victims of Gross and Systematic Violations, 16 *Hum. Rts. L. Rev.* 731 (2016).

27. Int'l Comm'n on Intervention and State Sovereignty, the Responsibility to Protect ¶ 6.12 (2001). 2005 World Summit Outcome, GA Res. 60/1, ¶ 138, UN Doc. A/RES/60/1 (Sept. 16, 2005) (establishing widespread state support for the principle of R2P); SC Res. 1674, ¶ 4, UN Doc. S/RES/ 1674 (Apr. 28, 2006); UN Secretary-General, *Implementing the Responsibility to Protect*, ¶¶ 8–9, UN Doc. A/63/677 (Jan. 12, 2009).

28. International Law Commission, Report on Work of Fifty-Third Session, UN GAOR, 56th Sess., Supp. No. 10, at 205, UN Doc. A/56/10 (2001). Natalino Ronzitti, *The Current Status of Legal Principles Prohibiting the Use of Force and Legal Justifications of the Use of Force*, Redefining Sovereignty, *supra* note 7, at pp. 91, 108–9: "A more acceptable proposal would be the adoption of a resolution by the Security Council

formulating criteria for intervention."; see, also, Christine Gray, *The Use and Abuse of the International Court of Justice: Cases Concerning the Use of Force after Nicaragua*, 14 EJIL 867 (2003).

29. See SC Res. 1973, UN Doc. S/RES/1973 (Mar. 17, 2011). But see Case Concerning the Military and Paramilitary Activities In and Against Nicaragua (*Nicaragua* v. *U.S.*) ICJ 134, ¶ 269 (1996). Before the UN Charter, the legality of humanitarian intervention was under debate with supporters relying on justifications of self-defense. But more than seventy-seven nations contested its legality, which the ICJ upheld in *Nicaragua*.

30. Alexander Orakhelashvili, *Collective Security* (Oxford University Press, 2011), pp. 168–9 (discussing the council's determination that the situations in Angola, DRC, and Haiti constituted threats to the peace while the situation in Zimbabwe did not). Michael Bothe et al., "Report from Rome on Redefining Sovereignty: The Use of Force after the End of the Cold War: New Options Lawful and Legitimate?" in *Redefining Sovereignty* at pp. 3, 4.

31. Anne-Marie Slaughter, *How the World Could—and Maybe Should—Intervene in Syria*, The Atlantic (Jan. 23, 2012) (citing Louise Arbour, President and CEO, International Crisis Group).

32. Lauterpacht, "The Grotian Tradition in International Law."

33. Cassese, p. lxxvii ("soul leaders" derives G.W.F. Hegel's definition of a *Welt-Historische Individuen* "world historical individuals" who are *Seelenführer* or spirit guides. See G.W.F., Hegel, Vorlesungen über die Philosophie der Weltgeschichte (1920 ed., pp. 77–8).

34. UN Charter, Art. 1, Purposes of and Principles of the United Nations, UN Charter, Art. 1.4: "To be a centre for harmonizing the actions of nations in the attainment of these common ends."

35. Raphael Lemkin, "IX: Genocide – A New Term and New Conception for Destruction of Nations," Axis Rule in Occupied Europe: Laws of Occupation – Analysis of Government – Proposals for Redress (1944) (reprinted in The Law Book Exchange, 2008).

36. *Akayesu*, Case No. ICTR-96-4-T, testimony by Witness J (Jan. 27, 1997).

Index